ULTIMATE MAUI

ULTIMATE MAUI

Ray Riegert

LESLIE HENRIQUES

Editorial Director

SANDRA WONG

Illustrator

ULYSSES PRESS

Published by: Ulysses Press
3286 Adeline Street, Suite 1
Berkeley, CA 94703

Library of Congress Catalog Card Number 91-65700

ISBN 0-915233-46-0

Printed in the U.S.A. by the George Banta Company

10 9 8 7 6 5 4 3 2 1

Managing Editor: Claire Chun
Editors: Sayre Van Young, Frances Bowles, Joanna Pearlman
Editorial Associates: Lee Micheaux, Andrea Orvik, Per Casey,
    William Kiester, Ellen Nidy
Cover Design: Bonnie Smetts, Leslie Henriques
Maps: Phil Gardner, Wendy Ann Logsdon
Index: Sayre Van Young
Researcher: Roger Rapoport
Cover Photography: front cover, Ivor Sharp/The Image Bank; back cover,
    Robert Holmes (top, bottom right) and Leslie Henriques (bottom left)
Color Separation: Twin Age Limited, Hong Kong

Distributed in the United States by Publishers Group West, in Canada by Raincoast Books, and in Great Britain and Europe by World Leisure Marketing

Printed on Recycled Paper

The authors and publisher have made every effort to ensure the accuracy of information contained in *Ultimate Maui*, but can accept no liability for any loss, injury or inconvenience sustained by any traveler as a result of information or advice contained in this guide.

For Alice, Keith and Leslie

Acknowledgments

The drawback to being acknowledged in a book about Maui is it means you worked in the office rather than Hawaii. That's not true of my wife, Leslie Henriques, who has been helping me research Maui for years; or Claire Chun who hails from Hawaii; or Roger Rapoport, who helped with the field research.

But editors Frances Bowles and Joanna Pearlman; indexer Sayre Van Young; and research associates Per Casey, Lee Micheaux, Ellen Nidy, Jennifer Wilkoff and Andrea Orvik would all I am sure happily trade this meager thanks for a plane ticket to paradise.

I am nevertheless extremely grateful to all of them and extend a huge *mahalo* to everyone who helped bring this book to press.

Contents

Ray Riegert's Best of Maui

ADVENTURES

Kayaking *(Page 37)*
Bicycling Haleakala *(Pages 40–41)*
Skindiving Molokini *(Page 138)*
Windsurfing Hookipa Beach *(Paia, page 153)*
Hiking into Haleakala Crater *(Pages 165–66)*

BEACHES

Kapalua Beach *(Kapalua, page 107)*
Napili Bay *(Napili, page 107)*
Makena Beach *(Makena, page 127)*
Red Sand Beach *(Hana, page 154)*

EXPERIENCES

Getting married *(Page 13)*
Touring Maui by helicopter *(Page 18)*
Whale-watching *(Pages 35–36)*
Seeing Haleakala at sunrise *(Page 164)*

HOTELS

Puamana *(Lahaina, page 81)*
Ritz-Carlton Kapalua *(Kapalua, page 95)*
Four Seasons Resort Wailea *(Wailea, page 117)*
Hotel Hana Maui *(Hana, page 147)*

RESTAURANTS

Gerard's Restaurant *(Lahaina, page 84)*
Roy's Kahana Bar and Grill *(Kahana, page 101)*
Raffles *(Wailea, page 121)*
Seasons *(Wailea, pages 121–22)*
Haliimaile General Store *(Haliimaile, pages 160–61)*

ROMANTIC PLACES

Swan Court *(Kaanapali, page 99)*
Kahakuloa *(Page 108)*
Hana *(Page 144)*
Waianapanapa State Park *(Hana, page 144)*

SHOPPING

Lahaina Printsellers *(Lahaina, page 86)*
Whalers Village *(Kaanapali, page 103)*
Elephant Walk *(Kaanapali, page 104)*
Kapalua Bay Hotel annex *(Kapalua, page 105)*
Hui Noeau Visual Arts Center *(Makawao, page 161)*

SIGHTSEEING SPOTS

Ahihi-Kinau Reserve *(Wailea, page 114)*
Bailey House Museum *(Wailuku, page 130)*
Iao Needle *(Wailuku, page, 132)*
Oheo Gulch *(Hana, pages 146, 154–55)*
Haleakala National Park *(Pages 162–66)*

THINGS TO DO WITH CHILDREN

Carthaginian II (Lahaina, page 76)
Sugar Cane Train *(Lahaina, page 79)*
Atlantis Submarine *(Lahaina, page 79)*
Hunting for Maui Diamonds *(Page 89)*
Whalers Village Museum *(Kaanapali, pages 91–92)*

VISTAS

Sunset at the Bay Club *(Kapalua, page 106)*
Keanae Peninsula *(Keanae, page 142)*
Nahiku *(Nahiku, pages 143–44)*
Haleakala Crater *(Page 164)*

Notes from the Publisher

An alert, adventurous reader is as important as a travel writer in keeping a guidebook up-to-date and accurate. So if you happen upon a great restaurant, discover an intriguing locale or (heaven forbid) find an error in the text, we'd appreciate hearing from you. Just write to:

Ulysses Press
3286 Adeline Street, Suite 1
Berkeley CA 94703

It is our desire as publishers to create guidebooks that are responsible as well as informative. We hope that our guidebooks treat the people, country and land we visit with respect. We ask that our readers do the same.

ONE

The Valley Isle

Residents of Maui, Hawaii's second-largest island, proudly describe their **1**
Valley Isle by explaining that "Maui *no ka oi*." Maui is the greatest.
During the last decade, few of the island's visitors have disputed the
claim. They return each year, lured by the enchantment of a place possessing 33 miles of public beaches, one of the world's largest dormant
volcanoes, beautiful people, a breeding ground for rare humpback whales
and a climate that varies from subtropic to subarctic.

Named after one of the most important demigods in the Polynesian
pantheon, Maui has retained its mythic aura. The island is famous as a chic
retreat and jet-set landing ground. To many people, Maui *is* Hawaii.

But to others, who have watched the rapid changes during the past
two decades, Maui is no longer the greatest. They point to the 2.3 million tourists (second only to Oahu) who visited during a recent year, to
the condominiums and resort hotels mushrooming along the prettiest
beaches and to the increasing traffic over once rural roads. And they
have a new slogan. "Maui is *pau*." Maui is finished. Overtouristed. Over-
populated. Overdeveloped.

Today, among the island's 92,000 population, it seems like every
other person is in the real estate business. On a land mass measuring 729
square miles, just half the size of Long Island, their goods are in short
supply. During the 1970s and 1980s, land prices shot up faster than
practically anywhere else in the country.

Yet over 75 percent of the island remains unpopulated. Despite pres-
sures from land speculation and a mondo-condo mentality, Maui still
offers exotic, untouched expanses for the explorer. Most development is
concentrated along the south and west coasts in Kihei, Wailea and Kaana-

pali. The rest of the island, though more populated than neighboring islands, is an adventurer's oasis.

The second-youngest island in the chain, Maui was created between one and two million years ago by two volcanoes. Haleakala, the larger, rises over 10,000 feet, and offers excellent hiking and camping within its gaping crater. The earlier of the two firepits created the West Maui Mountains, 5788 feet at their highest. Because of their relative age, and the fact they receive 400 inches of rainfall a year, they are more heavily eroded than the smooth surfaces of Haleakala. Between the two heights lies Central Maui, an isthmus formed when the volcanoes flowed together.

The twin cities of Kahului and Wailuku, Maui's commercial and civic centers, respectively, sit in this saddle. Most of the isthmus is planted in sugar, which became king in Maui after the decline of whaling in the 1860s. A road through the cane fields leads south to Kihei's sunsplashed resorts and beaches.

Another road loops around the West Maui Mountains. It passes prime whale-watching areas along the south coast and bisects Lahaina, an old whaling town that is now the island's sightseeing capital . Next to this time-worn harbor stretches the town of Kaanapali with its limitless beaches and endless condominiums. Past these glass-and-steel palisades, near the island's northwest tip, lie hidden beaches, overhanging cliffs and spectacular vistas.

The road girdling Haleakala's lower slopes passes equally beautiful areas. Along the rainswept northeast coast are sheer rock faces ribboned with waterfalls and gorges choked with tropic vegetation. The lush, somnolent town of Hana gives way along the southeast shore to a dry, unpopulated expanse ripe for exploration.

On the middle slopes of Haleakala, in Maui's Upcountry region, small farms dot the landscape. Here, in addition to guavas, avocados and lichee nuts, grow the sweet Kula onions for which the Valley Isle is famous.

Back in the days of California's gold rush, Maui found its own underground nuggets in potatoes: Countless bushels were grown in this area and shipped to a hungry San Francisco market. Today the crop is used to prepare Maui potato chips. With the possible exception of marijuana, these delicious snacks are the island's most renowned agricultural product.

Because of its strategic location between Oahu and Hawaii, Maui has played a vital role in Hawaiian history. Kahekili, Maui's last king, gained control of all the islands except Hawaii before being overwhelmed by Kamehameha in 1790. Lahaina, long a vacation spot for island rulers, became a political center under Hawaii's first three kings and an important commercial center soon after Captain Cook sighted the island in 1778. It served as a supply depot for ships, then as a port for sandalwood exports. By the 1840s, Lahaina was the world capital of whaling. Now, together with the other equally beautiful sections of the Valley Isle, it is a mecca for vacationers.

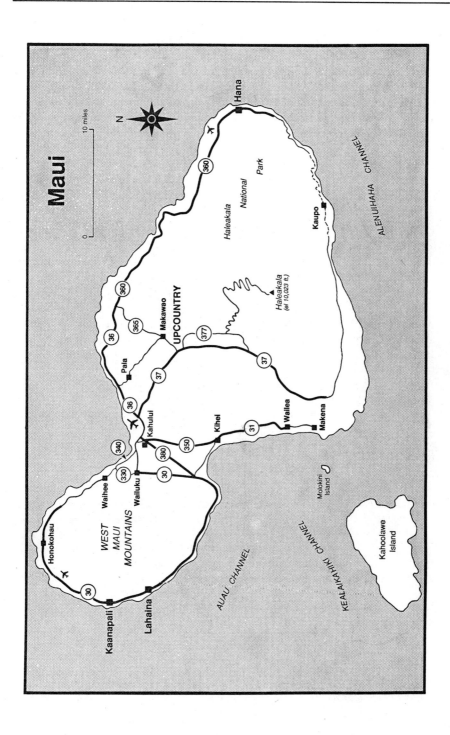

Maui's magic has cast a spell upon travelers all over the world, making the island a vacation paradise. Like most modern paradises, it is being steadily gilded in plastic and concrete. Yet much of the old charm remains. Some people even claim that the sun shines longer on the Valley Isle than any other place on earth. They point to the legend of the demigod Maui who created his own daylight savings by weaving a rope from his sister's pubic hair and lassoing the sun by its genitals. And many hope he has one last trick to perform, one that will slow the course of development just as he slowed the track of the sun.

Where to Go

Quite manageable in size, Maui is a destination that can be covered entirely in the course of a short vacation. Each of the island's regions has its strengths, and the areas with the most popular hotels and restaurants are not necessarily the best places for sightseeing. You may find yourself staying on one part of the island, visiting the beaches elsewhere and then setting off in yet another direction to tour.

Lahaina, the cultural heart of the island, is a falsefront whaling town that enjoyed its heyday in the 19th century and today remains rich in tradition. More than anywhere else on the island, Lahaina balances good restaurants and attractive lodgings with nightlife and shopping possibilities. It also offers a lengthy list of historic sightseeing spots.

MAUI THE GOD

So many legends have grown up around the demigod Maui, the island's namesake, that many believe the mischievous deity actually existed. Some even share the New Zealand Maori's view that Maui was instrumental in creating man. Part of Maui's appeal lies in his sense of humor. Every day was April Fool's Day for this merry prankster, who earned the monicker, "Maui of a thousand tricks."

According to popular legend, he created the Hawaiian chain by hooking the islands and pulling them up from the bottom of the ocean. It was also Maui who learned the secrets of firemaking from a mud hen and shared them with men and women across the island.

This Pacific Prometheus might still be with us today were it not for his determination to learn the secret of mortality from the goddess Hina-nui-te-po. To discover the truth, he entered the deity's mouth and dropped down into her stomach. After finding out her secret, he began crawling back up. But just as he was about to jump out with the sacred details, the goddess awoke and sliced Maui in half with her teeth.

During the Civil War, Union soldiers wore uniforms made of Maui cotton.

The neighboring **Kaanapali-Kapalua Area** is a stretch of dove-white sand that extends for miles along the southwest corner of the island. Some of Hawaii's prettiest beaches can be found along this corridor, along with one of the state's densest concentrations of hotels and condominiums. This is where most people stay, and where they spend luxurious days soaking up sunshine. Situated in the wind shadow of the West Maui Mountains, this area enjoys the island's best weather and offers Kodachrome views of Lanai and Molokai.

Hoteliers in the Kaanapali-Kapalua region will tell you that their biggest competitors have set up shop in the **Kihei-Wailea Area**, another strip with miles of pearly beach, this time lining Maui's southeastern quarter. Kihei, a perfect example of development run amuck, is a congeries of strip malls and condominiums. Wailea, on the other hand, is well-planned, a trimly manicured landscape dotted with scalloped beaches and five-star hotels.

The commercial center of the Valley Isle sits at the northern end of the isthmus separating the West Maui Mountains and Haleakala. The **Kahului-Wailuku Area** rises from Kahului Harbor, a major shipping area, uphill to the woodframe town of Wailuku. The seat of Maui County government, Wailuku, and neighboring Kahului, lack the beaches and physical appeal of the rest of the island, but offer visitors inexpensive hotels and restaurants.

Sightseeing is spelled with a capital "H" on the **Hana Highway**. Curving along the rain-doused northeastern coast, this magnificent drive curves past rainforests, seacliffs and checkerboard taro plantations to the idyllic village of Hana. Here you'll find friendly inns, a few restaurants and some of the most absorbing scenery in the islands. Local residents, looking out on the luxurious flora and tumbling terrain, lovingly call it "Heavenly Hana." It's not an exaggeration.

Maui's **Upcountry**, a band of ranchland that wraps around the lower slopes of Haleakala, is where the beach culture of the coast gives way to an Old-West society of cattlemen and Hawaiian-style cowboys, or *paniolos*. Angus and Hereford cattle roam these cool, moist slopes and eye-catching wildflowers grow with abandon.

You have to climb 10,000 feet, but upon arriving in **Haleakala National Park**, along the rim of Haleakala Crater, you may discover there is a place on Maui even more alluring than "Heavenly Hana." This is, after all, the "House of the Sun," a dormant volcano home to eerie occurrences and legendary sunrises. Often standing above the clouds and vaulting high beyond the surrounding countryside, Haleakala is definitely the place on Maui closest to heaven.

Climate

There are two types of seasons on Maui, one keyed to tourists and the other to the climate. The peak tourist seasons run from mid–December until Easter, then again from mid-June through Labor Day. Particularly around the Christmas holidays and in August, the visitor centers are crowded. Prices increase, hotel rooms and rental cars become harder to reserve and everything moves a bit more rapidly.

If you plan to explore the island during these seasons, make reservations several months in advance; actually, it's a good idea to make advance reservations whenever you visit. Without doubt, the off-season is the best time to hit the island. Not only are hotels more readily available, but campsites and hiking trails are also less crowded.

Climatologically, the ancient Hawaiians distinguished between two seasons—*kau*, or summer, and *hooilo*, or winter. Summer extends from May to October, when the sun is overhead and the temperatures are slightly higher. Winter brings more variable winds and cooler weather.

The important rule to remember about Maui's beautiful weather is that it changes very little from season to season but varies dramatically from place to place. The average yearly temperature is about 75°, and during the coldest weather in January and the warmest in August, the thermometer rarely moves more than 5° or 6° in either direction. Similarly, sea water temperatures range comfortably between 74° and 80° year-round.

A key aspect to this luxurious semitropical environment is the trade wind that blows with welcome regularity from the northeast, providing a natural form of air conditioning. When the trades stop blowing, they are sometimes replaced by *kona* winds carrying rain and humid weather from the southwest. These are most frequent in winter, when the island receives its heaviest rainfall.

While summer showers are less frequent and shorter in duration, winter storms are sometimes quite nasty. I've seen it pour for five consecutive days, until hiking trails disappeared and local streets were awash. If you visit in winter, particularly from December to March, you're risking the chance of rain.

A wonderful factor to remember through this wet weather is that if it's raining where you are, you can often simply go someplace else. And I don't mean another part of the world, or even a different island. Since the rains generally batter the northeastern section of the island, you can usually head over to the south or west coast for warm, sunny weather. Or if you seek cooler climes, head up to the mountains; for every thousand feet in elevation, the temperature drops about 3°. If you climb high enough on Maui, you might even encounter snow!

Calendar

Something else to consider in planning a visit to Maui is the amazing lineup of annual cultural events. For a thumbnail idea of what's happening when, check the calendar below. You might just find that special occasion to climax an already dynamic vacation.

JANUARY

Lahaina   The Lahaina Gallery sponsors a **Marine Art Festival** that combines art tours and whale-watching.

Kaanapali-Kapalua   Maui celebrates with music and dance at **Na Mele O Maui**, a festival held twice a year.

FEBRUARY

Kihei-Wailea   Top men and women golfers compete in the **Asahi Beer Kyosan Golf Tournament** at Wailea. The **Maui Marine Art Expo** at Stouffer's Wailea Beach Resort is an outstanding exhibition of marine painting, sculpture and mixed media held during the months of February and March.

MARCH

Throughout Maui   The **Marui O'Neill Pro Board Windsurfing Tournament** is a popular ten-day tournament staged in various locations around the Valley Isle.

Kaanapali-Kapalua   Hawaiian arts and crafts, music and dance are highlighted at the **Na Mele O Maui Festival** (also held in January).

Kahului-Wailuku   The **Maui Marathon** is run from the Maui Shopping Mall in Kahului to Whalers Village in Kaanapali in early March.

APRIL

Throughout Maui   Buddhist temples mark **Buddha Day**, the luminary's birthday, with special services. Included among the events are pageants, dances and flower festivals. Many of the activities occur at the Lahaina Jodo Mission.

Kahului-Wailuku   In early April, the Valley Isle Road Runners Association sponsors the **Iao Valley 10K Run**.

MAY

Throughout Maui   **Lei Day** is celebrated by people wearing flower leis and colorful Hawaiian garb. This island-wide festival featuring lei-making contests and Hawaiian entertainment is held on May 1.

Upcountry   **Seabury Hall Craft Fair** in Makawao offers local arts and crafts, food booths and live entertainment.

JUNE

Throughout Maui   **Kamehameha Day**, honoring Hawaii's first king, is celebrated June 11 with parades, chants, hula dances and exhibits.

Kaanapali-Kapalua   The **Kapalua Music Festival** features chamber music by internationally acclaimed artists.

Upcountry   Staged at the Eddie Tam Center in Makawao, the **Annual Upcountry Fair** is where the 4-H crowd swings into action. Enjoy the live entertainment and local delicacies and, if you're an aspiring performer, don't miss the Star Search.

JULY

Kaanapali-Kapalua   More than 100 different wines from California, Oregon and Washington, as well as Australia are sampled at the **Kapalua Wine Symposium**.

Kahului-Wailuku   The **Maui Jaycees Carnival**, akin to a county fair, comes to the Maui War Memorial Sports Complex in Wailuku. Local entertainment, games, rides and commercial booths are part of the fun. The Maui War Memorial Sports Complex also hosts the **Fourth of July Fireworks Extravaganza**, which features eats, explosives and live entertainment.

Upcountry   In addition to fireworks, Maui celebrates the Fourth of July with the **Makawao Rodeo**.

AUGUST

Throughout Maui   Buddhists perform colorful **Bon Dances** every weekend to honor the dead. On August 21, local residents celebrate **Admission Day**, the date in 1959 when Hawaii became the 50th state.

Kaanapali-Kapalua   In addition to a raw onion eating contest, you'll find food booths containing onion dishes from local restaurants, live music, a farmer's market and a cookoff where people can enter their favorite Maui onion recipe at the **Maui Onion Festival**, held at the Kaanapali Beach Resort.

SEPTEMBER

Throughout Maui   The highlight of Hawaii's cultural season is the **Aloha Week** festival, a series of week-long celebrations featuring parades, street parties and pageants.

Kaanapali-Kapalua   Hawaii's largest tennis purse is the prize on which everyone keeps their eyes at the **Kapalua Tennis Open Tournament**. A six-person relay across the nine-mile channel from Lanai to Kaanapali draws 50 international swimming teams to the **Maui Channel Relay Swim**.

Kahului-Wailuku The six-person **Hana Relay**, a 54-mile swim from Kahului to Hana, is one of autumn's more challenging events.

Hana Highway A popular event on the east side of the island is the **Haku Mele Celebration**. Staged in Hana's Plantation House, it provides yet another opportunity to enjoy traditional island entertainment and food.

Upcountry **Maui Cycle to the Sun** is the ultimate uphill challenge: a 38-mile bike ride from the ocean to the 10,023-foot peak of Haleakala. Covering the same route is the **Haleakala Run to the Sun**.

OCTOBER

Lahaina The **Lahaina Halloween Hoolaulea** is a memorable street party that includes a parade, food fair, music and dancing on Front Street.

Kaanapali-Kapalua The **Kaanapali Pro Am Golf Tournament** draws top stars from the PGA Tour.

Kahului-Wailuku The **Maui County Fair** features agricultural exhibits, ethnic foods and arts-and-crafts displays at the Kahului fairgrounds.

NOVEMBER

Kaanapali-Kapalua An $800,000 purse draws the best golfers on the professional tour to the **Kapalua International Golf Tournament**.

Kahului-Wailuku Hawaiian and other crafts are showcased at the **Lokahi Pacific Christmas Craft Fair**, held at the War Memorial Sports Complex in Wailuku.

Hana Highway The **Aloha Classic Windsurfing** competition at Hookipa Beach on the Hana Highway is the last of three events on the Pro Boardsailing Association World Tour.

Upcountry In Makawao, the **Maui County Rodeo Finals** bring together the top cowboys from Molokai and Maui.

DECEMBER

Throughout Maui Buddha's enlightenment is commemorated with **Bodhi Day** ceremonies and religious services.

Kihei-Wailea Santa is the center of attention at the **Wailea Christmas Festival**, staged in the Wailea Shopping Village.

Upcountry Christmas arts and crafts are the star attractions at the **Hui Noeau Christmas House** in Makawao.

The area code for all Maui listings in this book is 808.

Visitor Information

The **Hawaii Visitors Bureau**, a privately funded agency, is a valuable resource from which to obtain free information on Maui and the rest of Hawaii. With offices nationwide, the Bureau can help plan your trip and then offer advice once you reach Maui. The Valley Isle office is called the **Maui Visitors Bureau** (1727 Wili Pa Loop, Wailuku; 244-3530).

On the mainland, you can contact the Hawaii Visitors Bureau at the following offices: on the West Coast—at 3440 Wilshire Boulevard, #610, Los Angeles, CA 90010 (213-385-5301), or at 50 California Street, Suite 450, San Francisco, CA 94111 (415-392-8173); in the Midwest—at 180 North Michigan Avenue, #2210, Chicago, IL 60601 (312-236-0632); and on the East Coast—at 350 Fifth Avenue, Suite 808, New York, NY 10118 (212-947-0717).

Another excellent resource is the **Hawaii State Library Service**. With a network of libraries on Maui, this government agency provides facilities for residents and non-residents alike. The libraries are good places to find light beach-reading material as well as books on Hawaii. Visitors can check out books by simply applying for a library card with a valid identification card.

Planning Ahead

In planning a Maui sojourn, one potential moneysaver is the package tour, which combines air transportation with a hotel room and other amenities. Generally, it is a style of travel that I avoid. However, if you can find a package that provides air transportation, a hotel or condominium accommodation and a rental car, all at one low price—it is worth considering. Just try to avoid the packages that preplan your entire visit, dragging you around on air-conditioned tour buses. Look for the package that provides only the bare necessities, namely transportation and lodging, while allowing you the greatest freedom.

However you decide to go, be sure to consult a travel agent. They are professionals in the field, possessing the latest information on rates and facilities and their service to you is free.

Packing

When I get ready to pack for a trip, I sit down and make a list of everything I'll need. It's a very slow, exact procedure: I look in closets, drawers and shelves, and run through in my mind the activities in which I'll participate, determining which items are required for each. After all the planning is complete and when I have the entire inventory collected in one long list, I sit for a minute or two, basking in my wisdom and forethought.

Then I tear the hell out of the list, cut out the ridiculous items I'll never use, halve the number of spares among the necessary items and reduce the entire contents of my suitcase to the bare essentials.

Before I developed this packing technique, I once traveled overland from London to New Delhi carrying two suitcases and a knapsack. I lugged those damned bundles onto trains, buses, jitneys, taxis and rickshaws. When I reached Turkey, I started shipping things home, but by then I was buying so many market goods that it was all I could do to keep even.

I ended up carrying so much crap that one day, when I was sardined in a crowd pushing its way onto an Indian train, someone managed to pick my pocket. When I felt the wallet slipping out, not only was I unable to chase the culprit—I was so weighted down with baggage that I couldn't even turn around to see who was robbing me!

I'll never travel that way again, and neither should you. Particularly when visiting Hawaii, where the weather is mild, you should pack very light. The airlines permit two suitcases and a carry-on bag; try to take one suitcase and maybe an accessory bag that can double as a beach bag. Dress styles are very informal in the islands, and laundromats are frequent, so you don't need a broad range of clothing items, and you'll require very few extras among the essential items.

Remember, you're packing for a semitropical climate. Take along a sweater or light jacket for the mountains and something to protect against rain. But otherwise, all that travelers on Maui require are shorts, bathing suits, lightweight slacks, short-sleeved shirts and blouses and summer dresses or *muumuus.* Rarely do visitors require sport jackets or formal dresses. Wash-and-wear fabrics are the most convenient.

For footwear, I suggest soft, comfortable shoes. Low-cut hiking boots or tennis shoes are preferable for hiking; for beachgoing, there's nothing as good as sandals.

There are several other items to squeeze in the corners of your suitcase—suntan lotion, sunglasses, a towel and, of course, your copy of *Ultimate Maui.* You might also consider packing a mask, fins and snorkel and a camera.

If you plan on camping, you'll need most of the equipment required for mainland overnighting. On Maui, you can get along quite comfortably with a lightweight tent and sleeping bag. You'll also need a knap-

---

Maui must be an inviting place to visit—over 2.3 million travelers arrive on the Valley Isle every year.

---

sack, canteen, camp stove and fuel, mess kit, first-aid kit (with insect repellent, water purification tablets and Chapstick), toilet kit, a pocket knife, hat, waterproof matches, flashlight and ground cloth.

Lodging

Accommodations on Maui range from funky cottages to highrise condominiums. You'll find inexpensive family-run hotels, middle-class tourist facilities and world-class resorts.

Whichever you choose, there are a few guidelines to help save money. Try to visit during the off-season, avoiding the high-rate periods during the summer and from Christmas to Easter. Rooms with mountain views are less expensive than ocean view accommodations. Generally, the farther a hotel is from the beach, the less it costs. Another way to economize is by reserving a room with a kitchen. In any case, try to reserve far in advance.

Throughout this book, hotels are described according to price category. *Budget* hotels have rooms starting from $50 or less per night for two people. *Moderate* facilities begin somewhere between $50 and $90. *Deluxe* hotels offer rates starting from $90 to $130. *Ultra-deluxe* establishments rent accommodations at prices above $130.

Condominium Living

Many people visiting Maui, especially those traveling with families, find that condominiums are often cheaper than hotels. While some hotel rooms come with kitchenettes, few provide all the amenities of condominiums. A condo, in essence, is an apartment away from home. Designed as studio, one-, two- or three-bedroom apartments, they come equipped with full kitchen facilities and complete kitchenware collections. Many also feature washer-dryers, dishwashers, air conditioning, color televisions, telephones, lanais and community swimming pools. Utilizing the kitchen will save considerably on your food bill; by sharing the accommodations among several people, you'll also cut your lodging bill.

Restaurants

A few guidelines will help you chart a course through Maui's countless dining places. Each restaurant entry is described as budget, moderate, deluxe or ultra-deluxe in price. Dinner entrées at *budget* restaurants usually cost $8 or less. The ambience is informal café style and the crowd is often a local one. *Moderately* priced restaurants range between $8 and $16 at dinner and offer pleasant surroundings, a more varied menu and a slower pace. *Deluxe* establishments tab their entrées above $16, featuring sophisticated cuisines, plush decor and more personalized service. *Ultra-deluxe* restaurants generally price above $24 and the service is comparable to the food.

EVERYTHING BUT THE PROPOSAL

So many people get married on Maui that the island now has a Las Vegas-style wedding industry. All the major resorts and many condominiums offer honeymoon packages, and several hotels will even stage the blessed event. The price for eternal bliss ranges from $379 for the budget-conscious couple to $6200 for lovebirds with limitless dreams.

Typical is the **Westin Maui** *(2365 Kaanapali Parkway, Kaanapali; 667-2525), where the director of romance will do everything from arranging the blood tests to arranging the floral displays. Special packages include a minister, photographer and a traditional Hawaiian hair wreath (haku lei). Even the prayers are in Hawaiian.*

At the **Grand Wailea Resort and Spa** *(3850 Wailea Alanui Drive, Wailea; 875-1234) marriages are staged at the Seaside Chapel, a classic New England-style church complete with stained-glass windows. Sign up for the "Lei Aloha" wedding and you'll receive a memento painting from the artist who designed the chapel's stained glass.*

The **Maui Inter-Continental Resort** *(3700 Wailea Alanui Drive, Wailea; 879-1922) offers an "Orchid Rendezvous" complete with romantic dinner, massage for two and breakfast in bed. At the* **Four Seasons Resort Wailea** *(3900 Wailea Alanui Drive, Wailea; 874-8000), the "Romance For All Seasons" package includes a dozen long-stemmed roses, monogrammed terrycloth bathrobes and a limousine to carry you to a gourmet picnic.*

Perhaps the most extravagant wedding on the island is the "Journey into Paradise" at the **Hyatt Regency Maui** *(200 Nohea Kai Drive, Kaanapali; 661-1234). Performed in English and Hawaiian aboard a 55-foot catamaran, the ceremony is accompanied by slack key guitar and followed by a helicopter ride to Molokai and a wildlife safari.*

If you can't decide among all these outlandish options, simply pick up the phone and call **A Wedding Made In Paradise** *(Kihei; 879-3444). These ready-to-please consultants will help you choose the location and minister and even plan the ceremony.*

Family Travelers

Maui is an ideal vacation spot for family holidays. The pace is slow, the atmosphere casual. A few guidelines will help ensure that your trip to the islands brings out the joys rather than the strains of parenting, allowing everyone to get into the *aloha* spirit.

Use a travel agent to help with arrangements; they can reserve spacious bulkhead seats on airlines and determine which flights are least crowded. They can also seek out the best deals on inexpensive condominiums, saving you money on both room and board.

Planning the trip with your kids stimulates their imagination. Books about travel, airplane rides, beaches, whales, volcanoes and Hawaiiana help prepare even a two-year-old for an adventure. This preparation makes the "getting there" part of the trip more exciting for children of all ages.

And "getting there" means a long-distance flight. Plan to bring everything you need on board the plane—diapers, food, toys, books and extra clothing for kids and parents alike. I've found it helpful to carry a few new toys and books as treats to distract my son and daughter when they get bored. I also pack a few snacks.

Allow extra time to get places. Book reservations in advance and make sure that the hotel or condominium has the extra crib, cot or bed you require. It's smart to ask for a room at the end of the hall to cut down on noise. And when reserving a rental car, inquire to see if they provide car seats and if there is an added charge. Hawaii has a strictly enforced car seat law.

Besides the car seat you may have to bring along, also pack shorts and T-shirts, a sweater, sun hat, bathing suits, sun dresses and waterproof sandals. A stroller with sunshade for little ones helps on sightseeing sojourns; a shovel and pail are essential for sandcastle building. Most importantly, remember to bring a good sunblock. The quickest way to ruin a family vacation is with a bad sunburn. Also plan to bring indoor activities such as books and games for evenings and rainy days.

Most towns have stores that carry diapers, food and other essentials. However, prices are much higher in Hawaii. To economize, some people take along an extra suitcase filled with diapers and wipes, baby food, peanut butter and jelly, etc., etc.

A first-aid kit is always a good idea. Also check with your pediatrician for special medicines and dosages for colds and diarrhea. If your child does become sick or injured on Maui contact a local doctor or the **Maui Memorial Hospital** (242-2343). There's also a **Poison Control Center** in Honolulu, which can be reached at 800-362-3585.

Hotels often provide access to babysitters. In the Kaanapali area you can try **Babysitting Services of Maui** (661-0558) for bonded sitters.

Mermaid goddess Wewehi, sister of fire goddess Pele, resides in the waters off Maui. Keep an eye peeled for her. She's wearing limu-loloa, *a reddish-colored seaweed.*

Some resorts and hotels have daily programs for kids during the summer and holiday seasons. Hula lessons, *lei* making, storytelling, sandcastle building and various sports activities keep *keikis* (kids) over six happy while also giving Mom and Dad a break. As an added bonus, these resorts offer family plans, providing discounts for extra rooms or permitting children to share a room with their parents at no extra charge. Check with your travel agent.

Senior Travelers

Maui is a hospitable place for senior citizens to visit. Countless museums, historic sights and even restaurants and hotels offer senior discounts that can cut a substantial chunk off vacation costs. The national park system's Golden Age Passport, which must be applied for in person, allows free admission for anyone 62 and older to the national park facilities on the island.

The **American Association of Retired Persons** (AARP) (3200 East Carson Street, Lakewood, CA 90712; 310-496-2277) offers membership to anyone over 50. AARP's benefits include travel discounts with a number of firms; escorted tours and cruises are available through AARP Travel Experience/American Express (400 Pinnacle Way, Suite 450, Norcross, GA 30071; 800-927-0111).

Be extra careful about health matters. Consider carrying a medical record with you—including your medical history and current medical status as well as your doctor's name, phone number and address. Make sure your insurance covers you while you are away from home.

Women Traveling Alone

It is sad commentary on life in the United States, but women traveling alone must take precautions. It's entirely unwise to hitchhike and probably best to avoid inexpensive accommodations on the outskirts of town; the money saved does not outweigh the risk. Bed and breakfasts and good hotels are generally your safest bet for lodging.

The 92,000 people of Maui are a wonderful mix of racial groups. In fact, within the state of Hawaii, interracial marriages approach 50 percent.

If you are hassled or threatened in some way, never be afraid to scream for assistance. It's a good idea to carry change for a phone call. In case of an emergency, you can call the Sexual Assault Hotline at 808-242-4357.

Travelers with Disabilities

The **Commission on Persons with Disabilities** publishes a survey of the city, county, state and federal parks in Hawaii that are accessible to disabled people. For information, contact the Commission at 5 Waterfront Plaza, Suite 210, 500 Ala Moana Boulevard, Honolulu, HI 96813 (586-8121). You can pick up their "Aloha Guides to Accessibility," which covers Maui as well as the other islands, and gives information on various hotels, shopping centers and restaurants that are accessible.

The **Society for the Advancement of Travel for the Handicapped** (347 5th Avenue, #610, New York, NY, 10016; 212-447-7284) and the **Maui Center for Independent Living** (1464 D Lower Main Street, Room 105, Wailuku, HI 96793; 808-242-4966) offer information for travelers with disabilities. **Travelin' Talk** (P.O. Box 3534, Clarksville, TN 37043; 615-552-6670), a network of people and organizations, also provides assistance.

Be sure to check in advance when making room reservations. Some hotels feature facilities for those in wheelchairs.

Foreign Travelers

PASSPORTS AND VISAS   Most foreign visitors are required to have a passport and tourist visa to enter the United States. Contact your nearest United States Embassy or Consulate well in advance to obtain a visa and to check on any other entry requirements.

CUSTOMS REQUIREMENTS   Foreign travelers are allowed to bring in the following: $100 worth of duty-free gifts, and any amount of currency (amounts over US$10,000 require a form). Carry any prescription drugs in clearly marked containers; you may have to provide a written prescription or doctor's statement to clear customs.

DRIVING   If you plan to rent a car, an international driver's license should be obtained prior to arrival. Some rental car companies require both a foreign license and an international driver's license along with a major credit card, and require that the lessee be at least 25 years of age.

CURRENCY   American money is based on the dollar. Bills in the United States generally come in six denominations: $1, $5, $10, $20, $50 and $100. Every dollar is divided into 100 cents. Coins are the penny (1 cent), nickel (5 cents), dime (10 cents) and quarter (25 cents). You may not use foreign currency to purchase goods and services in the United States. Consider buying traveler's checks in dollar amounts. You may also use credit cards affiliated with an American company such as Interbank, Barclay Card, VISA and American Express.

WEIGHTS AND MEASUREMENTS   The United States uses the English system of weights and measures. American units and their metric equivalents are as follows: 1 inch = 2.5 centimeters; 1 foot = 0.3 meter; 1 yard = 0.9 meter; 1 mile = 1.6 kilometers; 1 ounce = 28 grams; 1 pound = 0.45 kilogram; 1 quart (liquid) = 0.9 liter.

Transportation

ARRIVING BY AIR

Chances are you'll be flying through Honolulu on your way into Maui. The **Honolulu International Airport** is served by American Airlines, Canadian Pacific Airlines, China Airlines, Continental Airlines, Delta Air Lines, Hawaiian Airlines, Korea Airlines, New Zealand Air, Northwest Airlines, Quantas, Philippine Airlines, TWA and United Airlines.

Three airports serve Maui—Kahului Airport, Kapalua-West Maui Airport and Hana Airport.

The **Kahului Airport** is the main landing facility and should be your destination if you're staying in the Central Maui region or on the southeast coast in the Kihei-Wailea area. United Airlines is the only carrier with nonstop service from the mainland. American Airlines and Delta Air Lines stop in Honolulu en route.

If you decide to land in Kahului, you'll arrive at a bustling airport that has been expanded. I never realized how popular Maui was until I first pushed through the mobs of new arrivals here. In addition to the masses, you'll find a coffee shop and lounge, snack bar, newsstand, gift shop, lei stand, information booth (872-3893) and baggage service.

Kapalua-West Maui Airport serves the Lahaina-Kaanapali area. Hawaiian Airlines and Aloha Island Air fly into the facility, which features a snack bar and sundries shop.

Hana Airport, really only a short landing strip and a one-room terminal, sits near the ocean in Maui's lush northeastern corner. Only Aloha Island Air lands in this isolated community. And don't expect very much ground transportation waiting for you. There is no bus service, though there is a car rental agency.

During the 19th century, sleek clipper ships sailed from the West Coast to Hawaii in about 11 days. Today, you'll be traveling by a less romantic but far swifter conveyance—the jet plane. Rather than days at sea, it will be about five hours in the air from California, nine hours from Chicago or around 11 hours if you're coming from New York.

Whichever carrier you choose, ask for the economy or excursion fare and try to fly during the week; weekend flights are generally higher in price. To qualify for lower price fares, it is sometimes necessary to book your flight two weeks in advance and to stay in the islands at least one week. Generally, however, the restrictions are minimal. Children under two years of age can fly for free, but they will not have a seat of their own. Each passenger is permitted two large pieces of luggage plus a carry-on bag. Shipping a bike or surfboard will cost extra.

MAUI FROM ABOVE

Much of Maui's best scenery is reached via serpentine roads or steep mountain drives. While the views are stunning, the best way to get a bird's-eye view is from the air. Helicopters, fixed wing aircraft and gliders all make it easy to see the volcanic uplands, waterfall splashed cliffs and dreamy back country beaches.

Cardinal Helicopters (Kahului Airport; 877-2400) operates 45-minute to two-hour tours focusing on such destinations as Haleakala crater, Hana's rainforests and waterfalls. Papillon Helicopters (Kahului Heliport; 877-0022) offers a 30-minute tour of the West Maui Mountains featuring Waihee Valley and the Honokohau Valley, as well as the Kapalua and Kaanapali areas.

There's also a west Maui/Molokai flight highlighting the tallest waterfall in the state, Molokai's Kahiwa. Hawaii Helicopters (Kahului Heliport; 877-3900) offers tours ranging from 30 minutes to five hours. The longer tours stop in Hana for 45 minutes to three hours, offering a chance to explore this verdant area's beaches and waterfalls via van.

At American Pacific Air (Kahului Airport; 871-8115) you can choose between a 45-minute tour of West Maui or a one-hour-and-40-minute circle tour of the entire island aboard four- and six-seater Cessnas.

For aerobatic flights and scenic tours in an open cockpit aircraft, try Biplane Barnstormers (878-2860). Trips range from 20 minutes to an hour and 40 minutes and reach a wide variety of destinations around the island. A special 30-minute aerobatic flight, guaranteed to knock your socks off, includes barrel rolls, loops and four-leaf clovers.

GETTING BETWEEN ISLANDS

Since cruise ships are the only commercial boats serving Maui and all five of the other Hawaiian Islands, most of the transportation is by plane. **Aloha Airlines** and **Hawaiian Air**, the state's major carriers, provide frequent inter-island jet service. If you're looking for smooth, rapid, comfortable service, this is certainly it. You'll be buckled into your seat, offered a low-cost cocktail and whisked to your destination within about 20 minutes.

Without doubt, the best service aboard any inter-island carrier is on Aloha Airlines. They have an excellent reputation for flying on time. I give them my top recommendation.

Now that you know how to fly quickly and comfortably, let me tell you about the most exciting way to get from Honolulu to Maui or to fly from Maui to other neighbor islands. Several small airlines—such as **Aloha Island Air** and **Air Molokai**—fly twin-engine propeller planes. These small airplanes travel at low altitudes and moderate speeds over the islands. Next to chartering a helicopter, they are the finest way to see Hawaii from the air.

Hawaii's grand oceanliner tradition is carried on today by **American Hawaii Cruises** (550 Kearny Street, San Francisco, CA 94108; 800-765-7000). Sailing the *S.S. Independence* and the *S.S. Constitution*, they cruise the inter-island waters, docking at Maui, the Big Island, Kauai and Pier 2 in Honolulu. The cruises are week-long affairs that evoke memories of the old steamship era.

CAR RENTALS

Renting a car is as easy on Maui as anywhere. The island supports at least several rental agencies, which compete fiercely with one another in price and quality of service. So before renting, shop around: check the listings in this book, and also look for the special temporary offers that many rental companies sometimes feature.

There are several facts to remember when renting a car. First of all, a major credit card is very helpful; if you lack one, you'll often have to leave a cash deposit on the car. Also, some agencies don't rent at all to people under 25. Regardless of your age, many companies charge several dollars a day extra for insurance. The insurance is optional and expensive, but if you don't take it you're liable for the first several thousand dollars in accident damage. So before leaving home, check to see how much coverage your personal insurance policy provides for rental cars and, if necessary, have a clause added that will include rental car protection.

Rates fluctuate with the season; slack tourist seasons are great times for good deals. Also, three-day, weekly and monthly rates are almost always cheaper than daily rentals; cars with standard shifts are generally less than automatics; and compacts are more economical than the larger four-door models.

Naturally, the most convenient means of renting a car is through one of the outfits at the airport. The problem with these companies, however, is that you pay for the convenience. The airport car-rental agencies are as follows: **Andres Rent A Car** (877-5378), **Avis Rent A Car** (871-7575), **Budget Rent A Car** (871-8811), **Dollar Rent A Car** (877-2731), **Hertz Rent A Car** (877-5167) and **National Interrent** (871-8851).

Then there are the agencies located away from the airport. Some of them will provide airport pick-up service when your plane arrives. I recommend that you check in advance and reserve a car from an outfit that extends this service. The others might be a little cheaper, but I've never considered the inconvenience worth the savings. Without a ride you'll be confronted with the Catch-22 situation of getting to your car. Do you rent a car in which to pick up your rental car? Take a bus? Or are you supposed to hitchhike?

Enough said. The rental agencies outside the airport include several companies that rent older model cars at very competitive rates. Two of these are **Word of Mouth Rent A Used Car** (877-2436) and **VIP Car Rentals** (877-2054).

If you find yourself in the Lahaina-Kaanapali area wanting to rent a car, try **Avis Rent A Car** (661-4588), **Budget Rent A Car** (661-8721), **Dollar Rent A Car** (667-2651), **Hertz Rent A Car** (661-3195), **National Interrent** (667-9737), **Rainbow Rent A Car** (661-8734) or **Thrifty Rent A Car** (667-9541). Among these agencies, Dollar, Budget and Hertz are also located at the Kapalua West Maui Airport.

Dollar Rent A Car (248-8237) is the sole company in Hana.

Kihei is served by **Avis Rent A Car** (879-1980) and **Kihei Rent A Car** (879-7257).

Note: Many rental agencies will forbid you from driving the road around the West Maui Mountains and the road from Hana around the southeast side of the island.

JEEP RENTALS

Generally, I don't recommend renting a jeep. They're more expensive and less comfortable than automobiles, and won't get you to very many more interesting spots. If you hit the rainy season though, and want to explore the back roads, it can't hurt. Except in extremely wet weather when roads are muddy, all the places mentioned in this book can be reached by car.

If you'd like to arrive on Maui by boat, Sea Link of Hawaii (661-8397) provides round-trip service from Molokai aboard the 118-foot Maui Princess.

If, like most visitors to Maui, you arrive at the airport in Kahului, you certainly won't want for car rental agencies. There are quite a few with booths right at the airport. A number of others are located around town.

There are several companies on the island of Maui that rent four-wheel-drive vehicles. Among the outfits offering jeeps are **Adventures Rent A Jeep** (571 Haleakala Highway, Kahului; 877-6626) and **Budget Rent A Car** (871-8811 or 661-8721).

MOTOR SCOOTER RENTALS

A & B Moped Rental (3481 Lower Honoapiilani Road, Honokowai; 669-0027) rents mopeds by the hour, day or week. These vehicles provide an exhilarating and economical way to explore the area. Though they are not intended for long trips or busy roadways, they're ideal for short jaunts to the beach.

PUBLIC TRANSPORTATION

There is almost no general transportation on Maui and the little that is provided lies concentrated in one small sector of the island. The **Lahaina Express** (661-8748) travels between Lahaina and Kaanapali. Picking up the baton in Kaanapali, the **Kaanapali Trolley** (667-7411) runs through this popular resort area.

Outside the immediate Lahaina-Kaanapali area you'll have to rely on **Trans-Hawaiian** (877-7308). This well-known carrier operates shuttle services regularly from Kahului to Lahaina-Kaanapali for $13. **Akina Bus Service** runs from Kahului Airport to Kihei, Wailea and Makena and costs $12 per person.

TWO

The Land

Geography

Maui is part of the Hawaiian archipelago that stretches more than 1500 **23** miles across the North Pacific Ocean. Composed of 132 islands, Hawaii has eight major islands, including Maui, clustered at the southeastern end of the chain. Together these larger islands are about the size of Connecticut and Rhode Island combined. Only seven are inhabited: the eighth, Kahoolawe, serves as a bombing range for the U.S. Navy. Another island, Niihau, is privately owned and off-limits to the public.

Located 2500 miles southwest of Los Angeles, Maui is on the same 20th latitude as Hong Kong and Mexico City. It's two hours earlier in Maui than in Los Angeles, four hours before Chicago and five hours earlier than New York. Since Hawaii does not practice daylight-saving, this time difference becomes one hour greater during the summer months.

Maui in a sense, is a small continent. Volcanic mountains rise in the interior, while the coastline is fringed with coral reefs and white-sand beaches. The northeastern face, buffeted by trade winds, is the wet side. The contrast between this side and an island's southwestern sector is sometimes startling. Maui's Hana region, for instance, is one of the wettest spots in the United States, but the southern side of the island resembles Arizona. Dense rainforests in the northeast are teeming with exotic tropical plants, while across the island you're liable to see cactus growing in a barren landscape!

For years, sugar was king in Maui, the most lucrative part of the island's economy. Today, tourism is number one. More than 2.3 million travelers worldwide visit Maui every year. It's now a 10.9 billion-dollar business that expanded exponentially during the 1970s and 1980s.

Marijuana is now Hawaii's foremost cash crop, flourishing on Maui, Hawaii and Kauai and representing a 3.4 billion dollar business. Of course, no Chamber of Commerce report will list the demon weed as Hawaii's prime crop. Officially, sugar is still tops. While the $238 million sugar industry is small potatoes compared to tourism, Hawaii remains one of America's largest sugar-producing states. But sugar, like everything on Maui and elsewhere in the islands, is threatened by urban development. A ton of water is required to produce a pound of sugar.

Pineapple is another crop that's ailing. Stiff competition from the Philippines, where labor is cheap and easily exploitable, has reduced pineapple plantations on Maui and other islands to a few relatively small operations.

The islands also do a booming business in macadamia nuts, orchids, anthuriums, guava nectar and passion fruit juice. Together, these industries have created a strong economy in the 50th state. The per capita income on Maui and throughout Hawaii is greater than the national average, and the standard of living is generally higher.

Geology

More than 25 million years ago a fissure opened along the Pacific floor. Beneath tons of sea water molten lava poured from the rift. This liquid basalt, oozing from a hot spot in the earth's center, created a crater along the ocean bottom. As the tectonic plate that comprises the ocean floor drifted over the earth's hot spot, numerous other craters appeared. Slowly,

---

MAUI WOWIE

For decades, Maui has been known for its sparkling beaches and lofty volcanoes. Agriculturally, the island has grown famous by producing sugarcane and pineapples. But during the past several decades, Maui and the other islands in the chain have become renowned for another crop, one that some deem a sacrament and others a sin.

In the islands it's commonly referred to as pakalolo. *Mainlanders know it more familiarly by the locales in which it grows—Maui Wowie, Kona Gold, Puna Butter and Kauai Buds. Because of Hawaii's lush tropical environment, marijuana grows year-round and has become the state's number-one cash crop (and one of its largest law enforcement problems).*

in the seemingly endless procession of geologic time, a chain of volcanic islands, stretching almost 2000 miles and including the idyllic island of Maui, emerged from the sea.

On the continents it was also a period of terrible upheaval. The Himalayas, Alps and Andes were rising, but these great chains would reach their peaks long before the Pacific mountains even touched sea level. Not until a few million years ago did these underwater volcanoes break the surface and become islands. By then, present-day plants and animals inhabited the earth, and apes were rapidly evolving into a new species.

Maui's first volcano, now the West Maui Mountains, rose above the waves about two million years ago. It was another million years before Haleakala first appeared. Gradually, lava flows from these two firepits joined together, creating the archipelago's second largest island.

For many millennia, the mountains continued to grow. The forces of erosion cut into them, creating knife-edged cliffs and deep valleys. Then plants began germinating: mosses and ferns, springing from windblown spores, were probably first, followed by seed plants carried by migrating birds and on ocean currents. The steep-walled valleys provided natural greenhouses in which unique species evolved, while transoceanic winds swept insects and other life from the continents.

Some islands never survived this birth process: the ocean simply washed them away. The first islands that did endure, at the northwestern end of the Hawaiian chain, proved to be the smallest. Today these islands, with the exception of Midway, are barren uninhabited atolls. The volcanoes of Maui and its sister islands, far to the southeast, became the mountainous archipelago generally known as the Hawaiian Islands.

Flora

Many of the plants you'll see on Maui are not indigenous. In fact, much of the lush vegetation of this tropical island found its way here from locations all over the world. Sea winds, birds and seafaring settlers brought many of the seeds, plants, flowers and trees from the islands of the South Pacific, as well as from other, more distant regions. Over time, some plants adapted to Maui's unique ecosystem and climate, creating strange new lineages and evolving into a completely new ecosystem. This process has long interested scientists, who call the Hawaiian Islands one of the best natural labs for studies of plant evolution.

With several distinct biological regions, there's much more to Maui than lush tropics. Rainforests give way to dry forests, and to coastal habitats where the vegetation is specially suited to withstand wind and salt. Higher in altitude are the bogs, pools of standing water containing rare life forms that have been forced to adapt to a difficult environment. Highest in altitude is the alpine zone, consisting of bare volcanic surfaces scattered with clumps of low-growing herbs and shrubs. Subzero temperatures, frost and even snow help keep this region desolate.

Sugarcane arrived in Hawaii with the first Polynesian settlers, who appreciated its sweet juices. By the late 1800s, sugarcane was well established as a lucrative crop. The pineapple was first planted on Maui in 1903 and the island now harvests over 50 percent of the state's pineapples. A member of the bromeliad family, this spiky plant is actually a collection of beautiful pink, blue and purple flowers, each of which develops into fruitlets. The pineapple is a collection of these fruitlets, grown together into a single fruit that takes 14 to 17 months to mature. Sugarcane and pineapple are still the main crops on Maui, although competition from other countries and environmental problems caused by pesticides have taken their toll.

Visitors to Maui will find the island a perpetual flower show. Two flowers the island is particularly known for are the protea and the carnation. Originally from Australia and South Africa, the protea comes in varying shapes, sizes and colors, each unique. They are found mostly on the leeward slopes of Haleakala, where the altitude, cool nights and dry volcanic soil provide the perfect growing conditions for this exotic plant. Carnations grow in abundance in the Kula area, where the fields are filled with color and the air is often heady with the flowers' distinctive perfume. But it is the sweetly scented plumeria, delicate orchids, exotic ginger, showy birds of paradise, highly fragrant gardenias and the brightly hued hibiscus that run riot on Maui and add color and fragrance to the

---

SAVE THE EAGLES (AND THE BIRDIES)

An environmental battle is brewing on Maui these days over a proposed golf course in Hana. Opponents argue that golf links mean fertilizers and insecticides. But several courses, including three in Kapalua, have already risen to the challenge, registering as participants in the Audubon Cooperative Sanctuary Program. That means they use organic fertilizers, employ biological controls to reduce turf stress and provide bird habitats and feeder boxes for local wildlife. Even the golfers are invited to contribute by participating in a bird census, logging species they see on a special "eagle and birdies" card.

Each Hawaiian island has its own official flower; the Valley Isle's blossom is the pink Maui rose.

island. Scarlet and purple bougainvillea vines, and the aromatic lantana, with its dense clusters of flowers, are also found in abundance.

One of Maui's unique plants is the silversword. Delicate looking, this silvery green plant is actually very hardy. It thrives on the moonscape of Haleakala, 6000 to 10,000 feet above sea level. Very adaptable, it can survive in extreme hot and cold temperatures with little moisture. Its silvery hairs reflect the sun and its leaves curl inward, protecting the stalk and creating a sort of bowl where rain is collected and stored. The plant lives from five to thirty years, waiting until the right moment before sprouting a three- to nine-foot stalk composed of hundreds of small, reddish flowers—and then it dies. In the same family as the sunflower, this particular type of silversword lives only on Haleakala and has been close to extinction for many years. Now protected, it is currently making a comeback.

Although many people equate the tropics with the swaying palm tree, Maui is home to a variety of exotic trees. The famed banyan tree, known for pillarlike aerial roots that grow vertically downward from the branches, spreads to form a natural canopy. When the roots touch the ground, they thicken, providing support for the tree's branches to continue expanding. The candlenut tree, originally brought to Hawaii from the South Pacific islands, is big, bushy and prized for its nuts, which can be used for oil or polished and strung together to make leis. With its cascades of bright yellow or pink flowers, the cassia tree earns its moniker—the shower tree. Covered with tiny pink blossoms, the canopied monkeypod tree has fernlike leaves that close up at night.

Found in a variety of shapes and sizes, the ubiquitous palm does indeed sway to the breezes on white-sand beaches, but it also comes in a short, stubby form featuring more frond than trunk. The fruit, or nuts, of these trees are prized for their oil, which can be utilized for making everything from margarine to soap. The wood (rattan for example) is often used for making furniture.

FRUITS AND VEGETABLES   There's a lot more to Maui's tropical wonderland than gorgeous flowers and overgrown rainforests. The island is also teeming with edible plants. Roots, fruits, vegetables, herbs and spices grow like weeds from the shoreline to the mountains. Following is a list of some of the more commonly found.

Avocado: Covered with either a tough green or purple skin, this pear-shaped fruit sometimes weighs as much as three pounds. It grows on ten- to forty-foot-high trees, and ripens from June through November.

Bamboo: The bamboo plant is actually a grass with a sweet root that is edible and a long stem frequently used for making furniture. Often exceeding eight feet in height, bamboo is green until picked, when it turns a golden brown.

Banana: Polynesians use banana trees not only for food but also for clothing, roofing, medicines, dyes and even alcohol. The fruit, which grows upside down on broad-leaved trees, can be harvested as soon as the first banana in the bunch turns yellow.

Breadfruit: This large round fruit grows on trees that reach up to 60 feet in height. Breadfruit must be boiled, baked or fried.

Coconut: The coconut tree is probably the most important plant in the entire Pacific. Every part of the towering palm is used. Most people are concerned only with the hard brown nut, which yields delicious milk as well as a tasty meat. If the coconut is still green, the meat is a succulent jellylike substance. Otherwise, it's a hard but delicious white rind.

Guava: A roundish yellow fruit that grows on a small shrub or tree, guavas are extremely abundant in the wild. They ripen between June and October.

Mango: Known as the king of fruits, the mango grows on tall shade trees. The oblong fruit ripens in the spring and summer.

Maui onion: Resembling an ordinary yellow onion in size and color, these bulbs are uncommonly sweet and mild. They are grown on the south side of Haleakala in rich volcanic soil, and enjoy enough sun and altitude to make them very sweet. A member of the lily family, the Maui onion is best eaten raw.

Mountain apple: This sweet fruit grows in damp, shaded valleys at an elevation of about 1800 feet. The flowers resemble fluffy crimson balls; the fruit, which ripens from July to December, is also a rich red color.

PRESERVING MAUI

With the current interest in ecology, even Maui's resorts are becoming environmentally aware. Most have instituted recycling and conservation programs. The Maui Land and Pineapple Company, owner of Kapalua, has asked the Nature Conservancy to manage 8000 acres on the slopes of Puu Kukui, a western Maui summit. The Kapalua Bay and Ritz-Carlton hotels offer an "eco-package," where a portion of each guest's bill is donated to preservation projects. Maui Inter-Continental Resort saves seven million gallons of water annually by recycling water and is replacing insecticides with potted citrosa plants that emit a natural mosquito repellent. Golf course trimmings that formerly went to the dump are now being composted and one hotel boasts a recycling program that handles 40 tons of glass and 46 tons of cardboard and paper each year.

Of Maui's 729 square miles, more than 75 percent is rural or wilderness.

Papaya: This delicious fruit, which is picked as it begins to turn yellow, grows on unbranched trees. The sweet flesh can be bright orange or coral pink in color. Summer is the peak harvesting season.

Passion fruit: Oval in shape, this tasty yellow fruit grows to a length of about two or three inches. It's produced on a vine and ripens in summer or fall.

Taro: The tuberous root of this Hawaiian staple is pounded, then made into a grayish purple paste known as *poi*. One of the most nutritious foods, it has a rather bland taste. The plant has wide, shiny, thick leaves with reddish stems; the root is white with purple veins.

Fauna

On Maui, it seems there is more wildlife in the water and air than on land. A scuba diver's paradise, the ocean is also a promised land for many other creatures. Coral, colorful fish and migrating whales are only part of this underwater community. Sadly, many of Hawaii's coral reefs have been dying mysteriously in the last few years. No one is sure why, but many believe this is partially due to runoff from pesticides used in agriculture.

For adventure lovers, Maui offers excellent opportunities for whale-watching. Every year, humpback whales converge in the warm waters off the island to give birth to their calves. They begin their migration in Alaska and can be spotted in Hawaiian waters from November through May. The humpback, named for its practice of showing its dorsal fin when diving, is quite easy to spy. Humpbacks feed in shallow waters, usually diving for periods of no longer than 15 minutes. They often sleep on the surface and breathe fairly frequently. Humpbacks are also quite playful, and are seen leaping, splashing and flapping their 15-foot tails over their backs. The best time for whale-watching is from January to April.

Unlike other whales, humpbacks have the ability to sing. Loud and powerful, their songs carry above and below the water for miles. The songs change every year, yet, incredibly, all the whales always seem to know the current one.

Maui is also home to many rare and endangered birds. Like the flora, the birds on this island are highly specialized. Hawaii's state bird, the nene, or Hawaiian goose, is a cousin to the Canadian goose and mates for life. Extinct on Maui for many years, several birds were reintroduced here in the late 1950s. There's still some doubt as to whether they'll survive on their own in the wild. The only place they currently live, besides the

Big Island, is on Haleakala. The slopes of Haleakala are also home to two other endangered birds: the crested honeycreeper and the parrotbill.

There *are* a few birds native to Hawaii that have thus far avoided the endangered species list. Two of the most common birds are the yellow-green *amakihi* and the red *iiwi*.

Known in Hawaiian mythology for its protective powers, the *pueo*, or Hawaiian owl, a brown-and-white-feathered bird, resides in Haleakala crater. The *koae kea*, or "tropic bird," also lives on Haleakala and in the crater. Resembling a seagull in size, it has a long, thin white tail and a striking striping pattern on the back of the wings.

Another common bird is the *iwa*, or frigate, a very large creature measuring three to four feet in length, with a wing span averaging seven feet. The males are solid black, while the females have a large white patch on their chest and tail. A predatory bird, they're easy to spot raiding the nesting colonies of other birds along the offshore rocks. If you see one, be careful not to point at it; legend has it that it's bad luck. Other birds that make Maui their home are the Hawaiian stilt and the Hawaiian coot—both water birds—along with the black noddy, American plover and wedge-tailed shearwater.

Not many wild four-footed creatures roam the island. Deer, feral goats and pigs were brought to the islands early on and have found a home in the forests. Some good news for people fearful of snakes: There is nary a serpent (or a sea serpent) on the island, although lizards such as skinks and geckos abound.

One can only hope that with the renewed interest in Hawaiian culture, and growing environmental awareness, Hawaii's plants and animals will continue to exist as they have for centuries.

The Sporting Life

SCUBA DIVING AND SNORKELING

Maui offers a wide variety of snorkeling and diving opportunities ranging from Black Rock off Kaanapali to Honolua Bay. While most of the dive operators are located near the island's south coast resorts, there are also good diving and snorkeling opportunities on the north shore at Paia's Baldwin Beach Park, as well as Hana's Waianapanapa State Park. From Maui it's also easy to reach neighboring destinations such as the Molokini Crater Marine Preserve and reefs off Lanai.

Extended Horizons (Mala Wharf, Lahaina; 667-0611) offers trips to Lanai for divers of varying abilities, as well as a variety of snorkeling trips. **Destination Pacific** (1223 Front Street, Lahaina; 669-3117) offers marine biologist-led dives to gems like the cathedrals of Lanai. Introductory courses, including free pool clinics, make it easy to learn how to explore the deep. **Ocean Riders Adventure Rafting** (Mala Wharf, Lahaina; 661-3586) specializes in all-day snorkeling trips to Lanai. **Lahaina Divers Inc.** (143 Dickenson Street, Lahaina; 661-4505) is another popular dive operator.

Underwater Habitat (36 Keala Place, Kihei; 879-3483) runs scuba and snorkeling trips off Wailea Point, Holoa Point and Molokini Crater. Certification classes and night dives are available. **Molokini Divers** (Kihei Boat Harbor, Kihei; 879-0055) features scuba and snorkeling trips to this popular islet. Visibility of 150 feet makes this marine preserve a great place to splash down. Another popular tour operator that also rents equipment is **Maui Dive Shop** (Azeka Place Shopping Center, South Kihei Road, Kihei, 879-3388; and Kihei Town Center, South Kihei Road, Kihei, 879-1919).

Popular with underwater photographers, **Mike Severns Diving** (Kihei Boat Ramp, Kihei; 879-6596) runs trips for certified divers to Molokini, Makena and Kahoolawe. His dives focus on the southwest rift of Haleakala, a fascinating place to study marine life. Led by informative biologists, these trips are an excellent way to see Maui's hidden marine life.

Maui Sun Divers (Kihei; 879-3337) provides all gear and offers everything from beginner trips to certification classes to night dives.

Interested in learning underwater photography? Sign on with **Ed Robinson's Diving Adventures** (Kihei; 879-3584). A prominent oceanic photographer, Robinson leads excursions aboard the *Seadiver II* and *Outrage* to the Lanai Cathedrals, Molokini and other popular dive sites.

SURFING AND WINDSURFING

If you must go down to the sea again, why not do it on a board. You'll find the best waves and winds on Maui's north and northwest shores. Popular spots include Hookipa Beach near Paia and Kanaha Beach Park in the Kahului area, as well as Napili Bay on the south coast. You can also take beginner lessons in the Lahaina area.

Mistral High Wind Center (261 Dairy Road, Kahului; 871-7753) is a full-service windsurfing school that can even plan complete windsurfing holidays. Similar opportunities await at **Windsurfing West** (460 Dairy Road, Kahului; 871-8733). Here the lessons include video replay (instant feedback) at the water's edge and are guaranteed to have you up and sailing in no time.

Thanks to a convenient radio communication system, instructors at **Maui Windsurfing Company** (520 Keolani Place, Kahului; 877-4816) remain in constant contact with their students. Lessons are at Kanaha Beach Park, which has a protected area ideal for beginners. Safe, onshore winds blow you back toward the beach. Rentals are also available.

Another good place to start is **Maui Surfing School** (adjacent to Lahaina Harbor; 875-0625). Andrea Thomas and her staff offer small classes and free board rental, and guarantee you'll be able to surf after one lesson.

The **Kaanapali Windsurfing School** (Whalers Village, Kaanapali; 667-1964) offers surfing and windsurfing lessons on the adjacent beach. Ninety-minute windsurfing lessons come with a guarantee of success. Four-person surfing classes are also offered, weather permitting. Rentals are available.

At **Maui Sailing Center** (101 North Kihei Road, Kihei; 879-5935) you can learn to windsurf off Maalaea Bay's Sugar Beach. Begin your lesson on a simulator and then master this fine art in the water accompanied by your instructor. Surfboard rentals are available, as well.

You can also rent or buy equipment at **Lightning Bolt** (55 Kaahumanu Avenue, Kahului; 877-3484), the oldest surf shop on Maui.

FISHING

Fishing in Hawaii is good year-round, and the offshore waters are crowded with many varieties of edible fish. For deep-sea fishing you'll have to charter a boat, and freshwater angling requires a license. For information on seasons, licenses and official regulations, check with the Aquatic Resources Division of the State Department of Land and Natural Resources.

RELATING TO THE OCEAN

For swimming, surfing and scuba diving, there's no place quite like Maui. With endless miles of white-sand beach, the island attracts aquatic enthusiasts from all over the world. They come to enjoy Maui's colorful coral reefs and matchless surf conditions.

Many water lovers, however, never realize how dangerous the sea can really be. Particularly in Hawaii, where waves can reach 30-foot heights and currents flow unobstructed for thousands of miles, the ocean is sometimes as treacherous as it is spectacular. Dozens of people drown every year in Hawaii, many others are dragged from the crushing surf with broken backs, and countless numbers sustain minor cuts and bruises.

These accidents can be entirely avoided if you approach the ocean with a respect for its power as well as an appreciation of its beauty. All you have to do is heed a few simple guidelines. First, never turn your back on the sea. Waves come in sets: one group may be small and quite harmless, but the next set could be large enough to sweep you out to sea. Never swim alone.

Don't try to surf, or even bodysurf, until you're familiar with the sports' techniques and precautionary measures. Be extremely careful when the surf is high.

Beaches and rocky points are usually good places to surf-cast; the best times are during the incoming and outgoing tides. Popular baits are octopus, eel, lobster, crab, frozen shrimp and sea worms. You can also fish with lures. The ancient Hawaiians used pearl shells to attract the fish and hooks, some made from human bones, to snare them. Your friends will probably be quite content to see you angling with store-bought artificial lures.

The deep blue sea around Maui can be nirvana for sportfishing. Choose between party boats, diesel cruisers and yachts custom-designed for trolling. All provide equipment and bait. Just bring your own food and drinks and you're in business. If it's not too rough, your skipper may head for the productive game fishing waters between Maui and the Big Island. If conditions are choppy, you're more likely to fish the leeward side of the island or off neighboring Lanai.

Ideal for groups up to four, **Robalo-One** (Lahaina Harbor; 661-0480) is a stable 23-foot vessel that hits speeds up to 40 miles per hour in pursuit of game fish. You'll catch snapper, wrasse, barracuda or jack crevalle on half-day trips.

Lucky Strike Charters (Lahaina; 661-4606) fishes for larger barracuda, shark, *ulua*, amberjack, *ono* and mahimahi swimming 150 feet below the surface. Combination trolling and bottom fishing is available.

Islander II and **Hinatea** (Lahaina Harbor; 667-7548) are matching sportfishing boats offering identical trips into coastal waters. On half- and full-day trips you'll fish for marlin, tuna, mahimahi, wahoo and shark.

If you get caught in a rip current, don't swim against it: swim across it, parallel to the shore. These currents, running from the shore out to sea, can often be spotted by their ragged-looking surface water and foamy edges.

Around coral reefs, wear something to protect your feet against coral cuts. Recommended are the inexpensive Japanese tabis, or reef slippers. If you do sustain a coral cut, clean it with hydrogen peroxide, then apply an antiseptic or antibiotic substance. This is also a good procedure for octopus bites.

When stung by a Portuguese man-of-war or a jellyfish, mix unseasoned meat tenderizer with alcohol, leave it on the sting for ten or twenty minutes, then rinse it off with alcohol. The old Hawaiian remedies, which are reputedly quite effective, involve applying urine or green papaya.

If you step on the sharp, painful spines of a sea urchin, soak the affected area in very hot water for 15 to 90 minutes. Another remedy calls for applying urine or undiluted vinegar. If any of these preliminary treatments do not work, consult a doctor.

Oh, one last thing. The chances of encountering a shark are about as likely as sighting a UFO. But should you meet one of these ominous creatures, stay calm. He'll be no happier to see you than you are to confront him. Simply swim quietly to shore. By the time you make it back to terra firma, you'll have one hell of a story to tell.

In the Kihei area, contact **Carol Ann Charters** (Maalea Harbor; 877-2181) for half- and full-day fishing trips great for catching marlin, tuna, mahimahi and *ono*. Choose between light or heavy tackle with **Rascal Charters** (Maalaea Harbor; 874-8633) when you fish for ahi, *ono*, mahimahi and marlin. Half- and full-day trips aboard a 31-foot vessel include game and bottom fishing.

There is also good fishing from the shore in many places. *Ulua, papio* and threadfin are the most common catches, but you'll also find goatfish, triggerfish, leatherback, milkfish, *moano*, big-eyed scad, bonefish, mullet and mountain bass. For information on the best places for offshore fishing, ask at local fishing stores, or try the following beaches: Hoaluha Park, Launiupoko State Wayside Park, Honokawai Beach Park, D.T. Fleming Park, Honokahau Beach, Keawakapu Beach, Poolenalena Beach Park, Black Sands Beach, Little Beach and Waianapanapa State Park.

TORCHFISHING

The old Hawaiians often fished at night by torchlight. They fashioned torches by inserting nuts from the *kukui* tree into the hollow end of a bamboo pole, then lighting the flammable nuts. When fish swam like moths to the flame, the Hawaiians speared, clubbed or netted them. Today, locals use flashlights.

CRABBING

There are two important crab species in Hawaii—Kona crabs and Samoan crabs. The Kona variety are found in relatively deep water, and can usually be caught only from a boat. Samoan crabs inhabit sandy and muddy areas in bays and near river mouths. All that most local people use to catch them is a net fastened to a round wire hoop and secured by a string. The net is lowered to the bottom; then, after a crab has gone for the bait, the entire contraption is raised to the surface.

SQUIDDING

Between June and December, squidding is a popular Hawaiian sport. Actually, the term is a misnomer: squid inhabit deep water and are not usually hunted. What you'll really be after are octopuses. There are two varieties in Hawaii, both of which are commonly found in water three or four feet deep: the *hee*, a grayish-brown animal that changes color like a chameleon, and the *puloa*, a red-colored mollusk with white stripes on its head. Both are nocturnal and live in holes along coral reefs. The Hawaiians used to pick the octopus up, letting it cling to their chest and shoulders. When they were ready to bag their prize, they'd dispatch the creature by biting it between the eyes. Today, most people feel more comfortable spearing the beast.

SHELLFISH GATHERING

Among Hawaii's many natural food sources are the shellfish that inhabit coastal waters. Oysters and clams, which use their muscular feet to burrow into sand and soft mud, are collected along the bottom of Hawaii's bays. Lobsters, though illegal to spear, are taken with short poles to which cable leaders and baited hooks are attached. Local people also gather limpets. These tiny black shellfish, locally known as *opihi*, cling tenaciously to rocks in areas of very rough surf. The Hawaiians gather them by leaping into the water after one set of waves breaks, then jumping out before the next set arrives. Being a coward myself, I simply order them in Hawaiian restaurants.

SAILING AND WHALE-WATCHING

Eager to protect the whales who winter in these waters, local officials have forced power craft to keep their distance from these cetaceans. But these restrictions are not so severe as to unduly interfere with the many sailing vessels that offer whale-watching opportunities off the Maui coast. You can also enjoy dive trips or pure performance rides on these beautiful vessels.

Sentinel Yacht Charters (Lahaina Harbor; 661-8110) specializes in six-person whale-watching trips aboard a 41-foot sloop, as well as snorkeling excursions, sunset trips and joysailing. Special trips include Molokai and Lanai. **Scotch Mist Sailing Charters** (Lahaina Harbor; 661-0386) offers half-day snorkeling trips to Lanai, as well as trips to the coral gardens of west Maui. Whale-watching and champagne sunset sails are

---

SEAWEED GATHERING

Few westerners think of seaweed as food, but it's very popular today among the Japanese, and it once served as an integral part of the Hawaiian diet. It's extremely nutritious, easy to gather and very plentiful.

Rocky shores are the best places to find the edible species of seaweed. Some of them float in to shore and can be picked up; other species cling stubbornly to rocks and must be freed with a knife; still others grow in sand or mud. Low tide is the best time to collect seaweed: more plants are exposed, and some can be taken without even getting your feet wet.

also available. **First Class** (Lahaina Harbor; 667-7733) runs both snor-keling and performance sailing trips.

Windjammer Cruises (505 Front Street, Lahaina; 661-8600) has a 70-foot, three-masted schooner ideal for sunset dinner sails. You can dine on island cuisine, listen to live Polynesian entertainment and take in the views of Kahoolawe, Molokai and Lanai. Or, for a more intimate experience, try the six-passenger **Cinderella** (Maalea Harbor; 242-2779), a 50-foot yacht.

Kapalua Kai (Kapalua Bay; 669-4665) is a popular catamaran offering picnic-and-snorkeling and sunset sails. It sails Maui's most scenic waters and features whale-watching excursions in winter months.

Trilogy Excursions (180 Lahainaluna Road, Lahaina; 661-4743) receives high praise from repeat clients who climb aboard the 50-foot catamaran for excursions to Lanai. Once on the nearby island, they can swim and snorkel Hulopoe Bay Marine Reserve, enjoy a Hawaiian bar-becue and tour Lanai City.

PARASAILING AND HANG GLIDING

Lahaina and Kaanapali Beach are ideal places to become airborne. Wonderful views of Maui's west side and neighboring Molokai add to the fun. The typical parasailing trip includes 30 to 45 minutes shuttling out and back to the launch point and eight to ten minutes in the air.

Parasail Kaanapali (Lahaina Harbor; 669-6555) riders rise as high as 900 feet. **West Maui Parasail** (Lahaina Harbor; 661-4060) offers similar trips. **UFO Parasailing** (Whalers Village, Kaanapali; 661-7836) lets you ascend up to 600 feet and, if you wish, fly with a companion. For hang gliding from some of the most beautiful spots on the island, try **Hang Gliding Maui** (Pukalani; 572-6557).

MAUI: THE IDEAL CROW'S NEST

*About 1500 to 3500 of the world's 7000 humpbacks make the annual migration to Lahaina each year. Several local organizations study these leviathans and serve as excellent information sources. The **Pacific Whale Foundation** can be contacted at 879-8861 (or call their whale hotline at 800-942-5311). They also issue daily reports over local radio stations.*

A prime area for whale-watching lies along Honoapiilani Highway between Maalea Bay and Lahaina, particularly at McGregor Point. So while you're visiting Maui, always keep an eye peeled seaward for vaporous spume and a rolling hump. The place you're standing might suddenly become an ideal crow's nest.

Maui has more miles of swimmable beach than any of the other islands in the chain.

KAYAKING

A sport that's growing in popularity, kayaking is an exciting way to explore the waters. A good place to learn this adventure sport is **Ocean Kayaking** (158 Nanakila Place, Kihei; 874-7652). Guided tours include the Makena-La Perouse area on Maui's south shore, a north shore tour exploring the Honolua Bay/Honokohau area and a sunset excursion along Papawai Point. Along the way you might spot dolphins, flying fish or whales. In the Kihei area, **Maui Kayaks** (50-J Waiohuli Street, Kihei; 874-3536) offers half- and full-day tours that include snorkeling and whale-watching. Kayaks are also available from **Kaanapali Windsurfing School** (Whalers Village, Kaanapali; 667-1964).

Maui Sea Kayaking (Puunene; 572-6299) specializes in day trips to Maui and Lanai and full-moon trips to Molokini. Or they'll lead you on an overnight retreat for which a guide will arrange a seaside campsite, then return in the morning to prepare your breakfast and lead the way back to civilization. They also lead surfers to off-the-beaten-track beaches inaccessible by car.

Kayak rentals and tours can also be arranged through **South Pacific Kayaks** (2439 South Kihei Road, Kihei, 875-4848; and 505 Front Street, Lahaina, 661-8400). On their guided trips you're likely to see whales, sea turtles and dolphins.

RAFTING

Rafting trips are the adventurous way to enjoy the Maui coast. Easily combined with dive and whale-watching trips, these sturdy craft are a great way to reach hidden coves and beaches.

Hawaiian Rafting Adventures (1223 Front Street, Lahaina; 661-7333) operates half- and full-day trips to Lanai. Whale-watching trips are great fun in the winter months. **Ocean Riders Adventure Rafting** (Mala Wharf, Lahaina; 661-3586) will take you out to Lanai and, weather permitting, Molokai, for a glorious day of snorkeling. All trips are aboard rigid-hull inflatable boats. Another company offering tours is **Captain Steve's Rafting Excursions** (Lahaina Harbor; 667-5565), which heads out regularly in search of tropical fish, dolphins and exotic birdlife. One of their most popular trips circumnavigates Lanai. **Blue Water Rafting** (Kihei Boat Ramp, Kihei; 879-7238) offers both rafting and snorkeling trips to Molokini.

WATERSKIING

If you've always wanted to waterski in an island paradise consider **Ka-anapali Water Skiing** (164 Wahikuli Road, Lahaina; 661-3324). Equipment rentals are available here for a waterskiing adventure along this stunning coastline.

HORSEBACK RIDING

Maui's volcanic landscape, beaches and sculptured valleys are ideal sites for equestrian excursions. A variety of rides are available across the island—from the shoreline of Hana to the slopes of Haleakala, you can count on seeing wildlife, lava fields and great sunsets.

Hit the trail on Maui's north shore with **Adventures on Horseback** (Makawao; 242-7445) and you'll ride along 300-foot cliffs, see lush rainforests and take a break to swim in waterfall-fed pools.

Oheo Stables (Hana Highway, one mile south of National Park Headquarters at Seven Sacred Pools; 667-2222) offers two-and-a-half-hour excursions up the backside of Haleakala. Trips ascend through a tropical rainforest and include views of waterfalls and the Kipahulu Valley. Highlights include the view from Pipiwai lookout above Oheo Gulch.

Makena Stables (7299 Old Makena Road, Makena; 879-0244) leads trail rides across the scenic 30,000-acre Ulupalakua Ranch on the south slope of Haleakala. As you cross this rugged ranchland you may spot axis deer, Hawaiian owls and pheasants. Mountain trails cross a 200-year-old lava flow. Choose among three-hour, four-hour and all day rides, including one to the Tedeschi winery.

At **Thompson Ranch and Riding Stables** (Thompson Road, Kula; 878-1910) visitors ride through pastureland on short day and sunset rides that offer views of the other islands. The full-day Haleakala ride enters the crater at 10,000 feet.

For tours of Haleakala National Park, contact **Pony Express Tours** (667-2200), which leads half- and full-day horseback trips through the crater. **Charlie's Trail Rides and Pack Trips** (248-8209) leads overnight horseback trips from Kaupo through the crater.

GOLF

With more than a dozen public and private courses, Maui is golf heaven. Choices on the Valley Isle range from country club links to inexpensive community courses. Also, several resorts offer a choice of championship courses ideal for golfers looking for change of pace. These are open to the public for a hefty fee.

Three of the public tennis courts in Wailea are grass, the only public grass courts in the islands.

Waiehu Municipal Golf Course (Kahekili Highway, Waiehu; 243-7400) is the island's only publicly owned course. With a front nine on the shoreline and a challenging back nine along the mountains, this course offers plenty of variety. Other amenities include a driving range and practice green.

Sandalwood (2500 Honoapiilani Highway, Wailuku; 242-7090) is one of Maui's newest courses. Somewhat hilly, this par-72 course was designed by Nelson Wright. Four holes have lakes or ponds. There's a full-service restaurant and pro shop on the premises, as well as a practice range, a chipping green and three putting greens.

In the same area, the private **Waikapu Valley Country Club** (244-7090) is an 18-hole gem offering great ocean views. Water features abound on this course.

Designed by golf course architect Robert Trent Jones Sr., the **Royal Kaanapali Golf Courses** (Kaanapali Beach Resort, Kaanapali; 661-3691) are among the island's finest. The championship par-71 North Course has a slight incline. The easier South Course is intersected by Maui's popular sugarcane train.

With three courses, the **Kapalua Golf Club** (300 Kapalua Drive, Kapalua; 669-8044) is one of the best places to golf on Maui. For a real challenge, try the par-73 Plantation Course, built in the heart of pineapple country. The oceanfront Bay Course was created by Arnold Palmer himself. The Village Course ascends into the foothills.

The **Wailea Golf Club** (879-2966), located in the heart of the Wailea resort complex, offers two courses. The 18-hole "blue course" heads uphill along the slopes of Haleakala. The more challenging "orange course" has magnificent ocean views.

Located next to the Maui Prince Resort, **Makena Golf Course** (5415 Makena-Alanui Road, Wailea; 879-3344) is a fool's paradise with 64 traps waiting to trip you up. Rolling terrain and beautiful views of the neighbor islands make these links a treat. A second course opened here in 1993, making Makena one of Maui's prime golfing destinations.

The **Maui Country Club** (48 Nonohe Place, Paia; 877-7893) is a relatively easy nine-hole course open to the public on Mondays.

The upcountry **Pukalani Country Club** (360 Pukalani; 572-1314), on the slopes of Haleakala, is an 18-hole public course. Bring a jacket or sweater because these links can get cool or windy. Boasting the highest elevation of all Maui's courses, this one is a sleeper (with great views).

TENNIS

If you're an avid tennis fan, or just in the mood to whack a few balls, you're in luck. Public tennis courts are easily found throughout the island. Almost all are lighted and convenient to major resort destinations. In the Kahului area, try the courts at the **Kahului Community Center** (Onehu and Uhu streets) and the **Maui Community Center** (Kaahumanu and Wakea avenues). In Wailuku, try **Wailuku War Memorial** (1580 Kaahumanu Avenue), or the public courts at Wells and Market streets or on Onehee Street.

In the Lahaina area, you'll enjoy the courts at the **Lahaina Civic Center** (1840 Honoapiilani Highway) or at **Malu-ulu-olele Park** (Front and Shaw streets).

Kihei public courts are found at **Kalama Park** (Kihei Road) and **Maui Sunset Condominiums** (Waipulani Road).

Popular upcountry courts are found at the **Eddie Tam Memorial Center** in Makawao and the **Pukalani Community Center** in Pukalani. In the Hana area you can play at the **Hana Ball Park**.

For general information, call the County Department of Parks and Recreation at 243-7389 or the Hawaii Visitor's Bureau at 871-8691.

Hard-core tennis fans choose their Maui accommodations based on the tennis facilities. Some of the favorites, also open to the general public, include the **Makena Tennis Garden** (Makena Resort, 5400 Makena Alanui Drive, Makena; 879-8777), **Wailea Tennis Club** (131 Wailea Iki Place, Wailea; 879-1958), the **Hyatt Regency Maui** (200 Nohea Kai Drive, Kaanapali; 661-1234), **Maui Marriott** (100 Nohea Kai Drive, Kaanapali; 667-1200) and the **Kapalua Tennis Garden** (100 Kapalua Drive, Kapalua; 669-5677).

BICYCLING

If you've ever wanted to zip down a mountainside or go off-road in volcanic highlands, you've come to the right place. While Maui is best known for its downhill cycling trips, there are also many other challenging adventures. For example, you can enjoy the remote route from Hana to Ulupalakua or head from Kapalua to Wailuku via Kahakuloa.

Chris' Bike Adventures (Kula; 871-2453) runs such intriguing trips as the Haleakala Wine Trek, a tour of the mountain's remote backside and a trip along the island's hidden northwest coast, complete with off-road biking. Unlike other bike tours, this company lets riders bicycle at their own pace. Half- and full-day trips include gourmet lunch.

At **Maui Downhill** (199 Dairy Road, Kahului; 871-2155) you'll enjoy sunrise day-trips and mid-morning runs on Haleakala. The sunrise run is a beautiful 38-mile trip from the crater to sea level. Other, less

---

In 1976, a replica of an ancient Polynesian canoe, the Hokulea, *set sail from Maui for Tahiti, re-creating an ancestral voyage of the Hawaiian people.*

---

strenuous trails also offer great views of the mountain, ranchlands and verdant forests.

Similar trips are offered by **Cruiser Bob's Haleakala Downhill** (99 Hana Highway, Paia; 579-8444). Equipment includes full-face helmets, windbreaker pants and custom megabrakes.

Another company operating Haleakala downhill bike tours is **Maui Mountain Cruisers** (1700 Lower Kula Road, Makawao; 871-6014), which serves breakfast or lunch on morning or midday rides; the most popular trip circumnavigates neighboring Lanai.

For those of you who prefer to go it alone, **Fun Rentals** (193 Lahainaluna Road, Lahaina; 661-3053) rents mountain bikes and ten-speed cruisers. The **Bike Shop** has a store in Kahului (111 Hana Highway; 877-5848) that both rents and sells bikes and accessories, and also does repair work.

CAMPING

Camping on Maui usually means pitching a tent, reserving a cabin or renting a camper. Throughout the island there are secluded spots and beaches, and numerous county, state and federal parks. All the campsites, together with hiking trails, are described in the following chapters; it's a good idea to consult those detailed listings when planning your trip.

Before you set out to camp, there are a few very important matters that I want to explain more fully. First, bring a campstove: firewood is scarce in most areas and soaking wet in others.

Another problem that you're actually more likely to encounter are those nasty varmints that buzz in your ear just as you're falling asleep— mosquitoes. Maui contains neither snakes nor poison ivy, but it has plenty of these dive-bombing pests. Like me, you probably consider that it's always open season on the little bastards.

With most of the archipelago's other species, however, you'll have to be a careful conservationist. You'll be sharing the wilderness with pigs, goats, tropical birds, deer and mongooses, as well as a spectacular array of exotic and indigenous plants. They exist in one of the world's most delicate ecological balances. There are more endangered species in Hawaii than in all the rest of the United States. So keep in mind the maxim that the Hawaiians try to follow. *Ua mau ke ea o ka aina i ka pono:* The life of the land is preserved in righteousness.

Though extremely popular with adventurers, Maui has very few official campsites. The laws restricting camping here are more strictly enforced than on other islands. The emphasis on this boom island favors
condominiums and resort hotels rather than outdoor living, but you can
still escape the concrete congestion at several parks and unofficial campsites (including one of the most spectacular tenting areas in all Hawaii—
Haleakala Crater).

Camping at **county parks** requires a permit. These are issued for a
maximum of three nights at each campsite, and cost $3 per person per
night, children 50¢. Permits can be obtained at War Memorial Gym
adjacent to Baldwin High School, Route 32, Wailuku, or by writing the
Department of Parks and Recreation, Permit Department, 1580 Kaahumanu Avenue, Wailuku, Maui, HI 96793 (243-7389).

State park permits are free and allow camping for five days. They
can be obtained at the Division of State Parks in the State Building, High
Street, Wailuku, or by writing the Division of State Parks, 54 South
High Street, Wailuku, Maui, HI 96793 (243-5354). You can also rent
cabins at Wainapanapa and Polipoli state parks through this office.

If you plan on camping in Haleakala Crater, you must obtain a permit
on the day you are camping. You can do so at Haleakala National Park
headquarters, located on the way to the crater. These permits are allo-
cated on a first-come, first-served basis.

Remember, rainfall is heavy along the northeast shore around Hana,
but infrequent on the south coast. Also, Haleakala crater gets quite cold;
you'll need heavy clothing and sleeping gear.

It is best to bring along your own camping gear, but in a pinch check
Maui Expeditions (87 South Puunene Avenue, Kahului; 871-8787),
which sells and rents supplies. **Maui Sporting Goods** (92 North Market Street, Wailuku; 244-0011) has a large selection of gear for sale
while **Gaspro Inc.** (365 Hanakai Street, Kahului; 877-0056) sells a limited amount of camping equipment.

HIKING

Many people complain that Maui is overdeveloped. The wall-to-wall
condominiums lining the Kaanapali and Kihei beachfront can be pretty
depressing to the outdoors lover. But happily there is a way to escape.
Hike right out of it.

The Valley Isle has many fine trails that lead through Hana's rainforest,
Haleakala's magnificent crater, up to West Maui's peaks and across the
south shore's arid lava flows. Any of them will carry you far from the
madding crowd. It's quite simple on Maui to trade the tourist enclaves
for virgin mountains, untrammeled beaches and eerie volcanic terrain. One
note: A number of trails pass preserved cultural or historical sites. Please

do not disturb these in any way. For more information, contact the Division of Forestry and Wildlife, Na Ala Hele Trails and Access Program (54 South High Street, Room 101, Wailuku, HI 96793; 243-5352).

Most trails you'll be hiking are composed of volcanic rock. This is a very crumbly substance, so be extremely cautious when climbing rock faces. In fact, you should avoid steep climbs if possible. Stay on the trails: Maui's dense undergrowth makes it very easy to get lost. If you get lost at night, stay where you are. Because of the low latitude, night descends rapidly here; there's practically no twilight. Once darkness falls, it can be very dangerous to move around. You should also be careful to purify all drinking water. And be extremely cautious near streambeds as flash-flooding sometimes occurs, particularly on the windward coast. This is particularly true during the winter months, when heavy storms from the northeast lash the island.

It's advisable to wear long pants when hiking in order to protect your legs from rock outcroppings, insects and spiny plants. Also, if you're going to explore Haleakala volcano, be sure to bring cold-weather gear; temperatures are often significantly lower than at sea level and this peak occasionally receives snow.

You might want to obtain hiking maps; they are available from **Hawaii Geographic Maps & Books** (P.O. Box 1698, Honolulu, HI 96806; 538-3952).

If you're uncomfortable about exploring solo, you might consider an organized tour. The **National Park Service** (Haleakala National Park, Box 369, Makawao, Maui, HI 96768; 572-9306) provides information to hikers interested in exploring Haleakala or other sections of the island. What follows is a basic guide to most of Maui's major trails.

KAHULUI-WAILUKU AREA TRAILS   The main hiking trails in this Central Maui region lie in Iao Valley, Kahului and along Kakekili Highway (Route 340).

Iao Stream Trail (1 mile) leads from the Iao Valley State Monument parking lot for half a mile along the stream. The second half of the trek involves wading through the stream or hopping across the shoreline rocks. But your efforts will be rewarded with some excellent swimming holes en route. You might want to plan your time so you can relax and swim.

Not far from the Kahului Airport on Route 380, birdwatchers will be delighted to find a trail meandering through the Kahana Pond Wildlife Sanctuary. This jaunt follows two loop roads, each one mile long, and passes the natural habitat of the rare Hawaiian stilt and the Hawaiian coot. Permits are necessary from the State Division of Forestry (243-5352).

Northwest of Kahului, along the Kahekili Highway, are two trails well worth exploring, the **Waihee Ridge Trail** and **Kahakuloa Valley Trail**.

Waihee Ridge Trail (3 miles) begins just below Maluhia Boy Scout Camp outside the town of Waihee. The trail passes through a guava thicket and scrub forest and climbs 1500 feet en route to a peak over-looking West and Central Maui. The trail summit is equipped with a picnic table rest stop.

Kahakuloa Valley Trail (2 miles) requires driving over the rugged, dirt-road section of Kahekili Highway to the picturesque town of Ka-hakuloa. This is one of the most beautiful, untouched spots on Maui. The trail begins across the road from a schoolhouse and passes burial caves, stands of guava and passion fruit, and old agricultural terraces.

KIHEI-WAILEA AREA TRAILS   **King's Highway Coastal Trail** (5.5 miles) follows an ancient Hawaiian route over the 1790 lava flow and is considered a desert region. The trail begins near La Perouse Bay at the end of the rugged road that connects La Perouse Bay with Makena Beach and Wailea. It heads inland through groves of *kiawe* trees, then skirts the coast and finally leads to Kanaloa Point. From this point the trail contin-ues across private land. Because segments of the trail pass through the Ahihi-Kinau Natural Reserve, which has stricter regulations, call or write Na Ala Hele (above) for more information.

HANA HIGHWAY TRAILS   **Hana-Waianapanapa Coastal Trail** (3 miles), part of the ancient King's Highway, skirts the coastline be-tween Waianapanapa State Park and Hana Bay. Exercise extreme caution near the rocky shoreline and cliffs. The trail passes a *heiau*, sea arch, blowhole and numerous caves while winding through lush stands of *hala* trees.

Waimoku Falls Trail (Seven Pools Walk) (2 miles) leads from the bridge at Oheo Gulch up to Waimoku Falls. On the way, it goes by four pools and traverses a bamboo forest. (Mosquito repellent advised.) Con-tact Haleakala National Park Headquarters for information on this trail.

UPCOUNTRY TRAILS   The main trails in Maui's beautiful Upcountry lie on Haleakala's southern slopes. They branch out from Polipoli Spring State Recreation Area through the Kula and Kahikinui Forest Reserves.

Redwood Trail (1.7 miles) descends from Polipoli's 6200-foot ele-vation through impressive stands of redwoods to the ranger's cabin at 5300 feet. There is a dilapidated public shelter in the old CCC camp at trail's end. A four-wheel drive is required to reach the trailhead.

Plum Trail (2.3 miles) begins at the CCC camp and climbs gently south to Haleakala Ridge Trail. The route passes plum trees as well as stands of ash, redwood and sugi pine. There are shelters at both ends of the trail.

Tie Trail (0.5 mile) descends 500 feet through cedar, ash and sugi pine groves to link Redwood and Plum Trails. There is a shelter at the Redwood junction.

Polipoli Trail (0.6 mile) cuts through cypress, cedars and pines en route from Polipoli Campground to Haleakala Ridge Trail.

Boundary Trail (4.4 miles) begins at the cattle guard marking the Kula Forest Reserve boundary along the road to Polipoli. It crosses numerous gulches planted in cedar, eucalyptus and pine. The trail terminates at the ranger's cabin.

Waiohuli Trail (1.4 miles) descends 800 feet from Polipoli Road to join Boundary Trail. Along the way it passes young pine and grasslands, then drops down through groves of cedar, redwood and ash. There is a shelter at the Boundary Trail junction.

Skyline Road (6.5 miles) begins at 9750 feet, near the top of Haleakala's southwest rift, and descends more than 3000 feet to the top of Haleakala Ridge Trail. The trail passes a rugged, treeless area resembling the moon's surface. Then it drops below timberline at 8600 feet and eventually into dense scrub. The unobstructed views of Maui and the neighboring islands are awesome. Bring your own water.

Haleakala Ridge Trail (1.6 miles) starts from Skyline Trail's terminus at 6550 feet and descends along Haleakala's southwest rift to 5600 feet. There are spectacular views in all directions and a shelter at trail's end.

(For Haleakala Crater trails, see Chapter Nine.)

THREE

History and Culture

History

POLYNESIAN ARRIVAL

The history of Maui, elegant and elaborate as it is, actually began after **47** that of other islands in the chain. Perhaps as early as the third century, Polynesians sailing from the Marquesas Islands, and then later from Tahiti, landed near the southern tip of the Big Island. By about 800 A.D., Polynesians from the Marquesas and Society Islands arrived on Maui. In Europe, mariners were rarely venturing outside the Mediterranean Sea, and it would be centuries before Columbus happened upon the New World. Yet in the Pacific, entire families were crossing 2500 miles of untracked ocean in hand-carved canoes with sails woven from coconut fibers. The boats were impressive structures, catamaran-like vessels with a cabin built on the platform between the wooden hulls. Some were a hundred feet long and could do twenty knots, making the trip to Hawaii in a month.

The Polynesians had originally come from the coast of Asia about 3000 years before. They had migrated through Indonesia, then pressed inexorably eastward, leapfrogging across archipelagoes until they finally reached the last chain, the most remote—Hawaii.

These Pacific migrants were undoubtedly the greatest sailors of their day and stand among the finest in history. When close to land they could smell it, taste it in the seawater, see it in a lagoon's turquoise reflection on the clouds above an island. They knew the courses of 150 stars. From the color of the water they determined ocean depths and current directions. They had no charts, no compasses, no sextants; sailing directions were simply recorded in legends and chants. Yet Polynesians discovered the Pacific, from Indonesia to Easter Island, from New Zealand to Hawaii. They made the Vikings and Phoenicians look like landlubbers.

On Maui, the seaborne colonizers established a line of kings who ruled the island for several centuries. Among them was Hua, a 12th-century monarch who earned a reputation for being a fierce warrior. According to legend, he angered the Hawaiian gods by murdering a priest and felt the holy wrath in the form of an island-wide drought. In desperation, Hua moved to the Big Island in search of fresh water, but the gods made sure the drought traveled with him.

CAPTAIN COOK

They were high islands, rising in the northeast as the sun broke across the Pacific. First one, then a second, and finally, as the tall-masted ships drifted west, a third island loomed before them. Landfall! The British crew was ecstatic. It meant fresh water, tropical fruits, solid ground on which to set their boots, and a chance to carouse with the native women. For their captain, James Cook, it was another in an amazing career of discoveries. The man whom many call history's greatest explorer was about to land in one of the last spots on earth to be discovered by the West.

He would name the place for his patron, the British earl who became famous by pressing a meal between two crusts of bread. The Sandwich Islands. Later they would be called Owhyhee, and eventually, as the Western tongue glided around the uncharted edges of a foreign language, Hawaii.

It was January 1778. The English army was battling a ragtag band of revolutionaries for control of the American colonies, and the British Empire was still basking in a sun that never set. The Pacific had been opened to Western powers over two centuries before, when a Portuguese sailor named Magellan crossed it. Since then, the British, French, Dutch and Spanish had tracked through in search of future colonies.

They happened upon Samoa, Fiji, Tahiti and the other islands that spread across this third of the globe, but somehow they had never sighted Hawaii. Even when Cook finally spied it, he little realized how important a find he had made. Hawaii, quite literally, was a jewel in the ocean, rich in fragrant sandalwood, ripe for agricultural exploitation and crowded with sea life. But it was the archipelago's isolation that would prove to be its greatest resource. Strategically situated between Asia and North America, it was the only place for thousands of miles to which whalers, merchants and bluejackets could repair for provisions and rest.

Cook was 49 years old when he shattered Hawaii's quiescence. The Englishman hadn't expected to find islands north of Tahiti. Quite frankly, he wasn't even trying. It was his third Pacific voyage and Cook was

Tourism, sugar, pineapple, cattle and agriculture are the island's five largest industries.

hunting bigger game, the fabled Northwest Passage that would link this ocean with the Atlantic.

But these mountainous islands were still an interesting find. He could see by the canoes venturing out to meet his ships that the lands were inhabited; when he finally put ashore on Kauai, Cook discovered a Polynesian society. He saw irrigated fields, domestic animals and high-towered temples. The women were bare-breasted, the men wore loincloths. As his crew bartered for pigs, fowls and bananas, he learned that the natives knew about metal and coveted iron like gold.

If iron was gold to these "Indians," then Cook was a god. He soon realized that his arrival had somehow been miraculously timed, coinciding with the Makahiki festival, a wild party celebrating the roving deity Lono whose return the Hawaiians had awaited for years. Cook was a strange white man sailing monstrous ships—obviously he was Lono. The Hawaiians gave him gifts, fell in his path and rose only at his insistence.

But even among religious crowds, fame is often fickle. After leaving Hawaii without ever visiting Maui, Cook sailed north to the Arctic Sea, where he failed to discover the Northwest Passage.

As the winter of 1778 approached, the British sea captain determined to steer a course south once more, spending the season in the Sandwich Islands. On November 25, at a latitude of 20° 55 ', as day broke across the Pacific, he first sighted Maui. To Western eyes it was an exotic locale, vaulting 10,000 feet above the waves with a peak that rose through the clouds.

By noon, canoes filled with local natives, including the great Maui chief, Kahekili, visited the English explorers, presenting them with elaborate feather cloaks and small pigs. By the next day, Cook had departed, sailing east to the Big Island.

He arrived at the tail end of another exhausting Makahiki festival. By then the Hawaiians had tired of his constant demands for provisions and were suffering from a new disease that was obviously carried by Lono's archangelic crew—syphilis. This Lono was proving to be something of a freeloader.

Tensions ran high. The Hawaiians stole a boat. Cook retaliated with gunfire. A scuffle broke out on the beach and in a sudden violent outburst, which surprised the islanders as much as the interlopers, the Hawaiians discovered that their god could bleed. The world's finest mariner lay face down in foot-deep water, stabbed and bludgeoned to death.

Cook's end marked the beginning of an era. He had put the Pacific on the map, his map, probing its expanses and defining its fringes. In

Hawaii he ended a thousand years of solitude. The archipelago's geographic isolation, which has always played a crucial role in Hawaii's development, had finally failed to protect it, and a second theme had come into play—the islands' vulnerability. Together with the region's "backwardness," these conditions would now mold Hawaii's history. All in turn would be shaped by another factor, one which James Cook had added to Hawaii's historic equation: the West.

KAMEHAMEHA AND KAAHUMANU

The next man whose star would rise above Hawaii was present at Cook's death. Some say he struck the Englishman, others that he took a lock of the great leader's hair and used its residual power, its mana, to become king of all Hawaii.

Kamehameha was a tall, muscular, unattractive man with a furrowed face, a lesser chief on the powerful island of Hawaii. When he began his career of conquest a few years after Cook's death, he was a mere upstart, an ambitious, arrogant young chief. But he fought with a general's skill and a warrior's cunning, often plunging into the midst of a melee. He had an astute sense of technology, an intuition that these new Western metals and firearms could make him a king.

In Kamehameha's early years, Maui and the other islands were composed of many fiefdoms. Several kings or great chiefs, continually warring among themselves, ruled individual islands. At times, a few kings would carve up one island or a lone king might seize several. Never had one monarch controlled all the islands.

Among the most powerful was the Maui chief, Kahekili. He was, according to the historian, Gavan Daws, "one of the last of the older generation of chiefs, raised in the tradition of warriors who roasted their enemies and used the skulls of the dead for filth pots." With the Valley Isle as a power base, he seized Oahu, torturing its chiefs and killing his own foster son. By 1786 he also controlled Molokai and Lanai.

During that same year, Captain Jean-François de La Pérouse, sailing under orders from the king of France, became the first Westerner to set foot on Maui.

Other players were entering the field: Westerners with ample firepower and towering ships. During the decade following Cook, only a handful arrived, mostly Englishmen and Americans, and they did not yet possess the influence they soon would wield. However, even a few foreigners were enough to upset the balance of power. They sold weapons and hardware to the great chiefs, making several of them more powerful than any of the others had ever been. War was imminent.

Kamehameha stood in the center of the hurricane. Like any leader suddenly caught up in the terrible momentum of history, he never quite

---

History cast Kamehameha the Great as the George Washington of Hawaii.

---

realized where he was going or how fast he was moving. And he cared little that he was being carried in part by westerners who would eventually want something for the ride. Kamehameha was no fool. If political expedience meant Western intrusion, then so be it. He had enemies among chiefs on the other islands; he needed the guns.

During the 1780s, Kahekili thwarted two attacks on Maui. But when two white men came into Kamehameha's camp in 1790, he had the military advisers to complement a fast expanding arsenal. Within months he cannonaded Maui. Attacking also with war canoes, he drove the forces of Kahekili's son, Kalanikupule, from Kahului up into the sharp-walled confines of Iao Valley.

In 1792, Kamehameha seized the Big Island by inviting his main rival to a peaceful parley, then slaying the hapless chief. By 1795, he had consolidated his control of Maui, grasped Molokai and Lanai, and begun reaching greedily toward Oahu. He struck rapidly, landing near Waikiki and sweeping inland, forcing his enemies to their deaths over the precipitous cliffs of the Nuuanu Pali.

The warrior had become a conqueror, establishing his new capital in Lahaina and controlling all the islands except Kauai, which he finally gained in 1810 by peaceful negotiation. Kamehameha proved to be as able a bureaucrat as he had been a general. He became a benevolent despot who, with the aid of an ever-increasing number of Western advisers, expanded Hawaii's commerce, brought peace to the islands and moved his people inexorably toward the modern age.

He came to be called Kamehameha the Great, a wise and resolute leader who gathered a war-torn archipelago into a kingdom. But with the revisionist history of the 1960s and 1970s, as Third World people questioned both the Western version of events and the virtues of progress, Kamehameha began to resemble Benedict Arnold. He was seen as an opportunist, a megalomaniac who permitted the Western powers their initial foothold in Hawaii. He used their technology and then, in the manner of great men who depend on stronger allies, was eventually used by them.

As long a shadow as Kamehameha cast across the islands, the event that most dramatically transformed Hawaiian society occurred after his death in 1819. The kingdom had passed to Kamehameha's son Liholiho, but Kamehameha's favorite wife, Kaahumanu, usurped the power. Liholiho was a prodigal son, dissolute, lacking self-certainty, a drunk. A native of Maui, Kaahumanu was a woman for all seasons, a canny politician who combined brilliance with boldness, the feminist of her day.

She had infuriated Kamehameha by eating forbidden foods and sleeping with other chiefs, even when he placed a taboo on her body and executed her lovers. She drank liquor, ran away, proved completely uncontrollable and won Kamehameha's love.

It was only natural that when he died, she would take his mana, or so she reckoned. Kaahumanu gravitated toward power with the drive of someone whom fate has unwisely denied. She carved her own destiny, announcing that Kamehameha's wish had been to give her a governmental voice. There would be a new post and she would fill it, becoming in a sense Hawaii's first prime minister.

And if the power, then the motion. Kaahumanu immediately marched against Hawaii's belief system, trying to topple the old idols. For years she had bristled under a polytheistic religion regulated by taboos, or *kapus*, which severely restricted women's rights. Now Kaahumanu urged the new king, Liholiho, to break a very strict *kapu* by sharing a meal with women.

Since the act might help consolidate Liholiho's position, it had a certain appeal to the king. Anyway, the *kapus* were weakening: these white men, coming now in ever greater numbers, defied them with impunity. Liholiho vacillated, went on a two-day drunk before gaining courage, then finally sat down to eat. It was a last supper, shattering an ancient creed and opening the way for a radically new divinity. As Kaahumanu had willed, the old order collapsed, taking away a vital part of island life and leaving the Hawaiians more exposed than ever to foreign influence.

Already Western practices were gaining hold. Commerce from Lahaina, Honolulu and other ports was booming. There was a fortune to be made dealing sandalwood to China-bound merchants, and the chiefs were forcing the common people to strip Hawaii's forests. The grueling labor might make the chiefs rich, but it gained the commoners little more than a barren landscape. Western diseases struck virulently. The Polynesians in Hawaii, who numbered 300,000 in Cook's time, were extremely susceptible. By 1866, their population had dwindled to less than 60,000. It was a difficult time for the Hawaiian people.

MISSIONARIES AND MERCHANTS

Hawaii was not long without organized religion. The same year that Kaahumanu shattered tradition, a group of New England missionaries boarded the brig *Thaddeus* for a voyage around Cape Horn. It was a young company—many were in their twenties or thirties—and included a doctor, a printer and several teachers. They were all strict Calvinists, fearful that the second coming was at hand and possessed of a mission. They were bound for a strange land called Hawaii, 18,000 miles away.

Hawaii, of course, was a lost paradise, a hellhole of sin and savagery where men slept with several wives and women neglected to wear dresses. To the missionaries, it mattered little that the Hawaiians had lived this way for centuries. The churchmen would save these heathens from hell's everlasting fire whether they liked it or not.

The delegation arrived in Kailua on the Big Island in 1820 and then spread out, establishing important missions in Lahaina and Honolulu. Soon they were building schools and churches, conducting services in Hawaiian and converting the natives to Christianity.

The missionaries rapidly became an integral part of Hawaii, despite the fact that they were a walking contradiction to everything Hawaiian. They were a contentious, self-righteous, fanatical people whose arrogance toward the Hawaiians blinded them to the beauty and wisdom of island lifestyles. Where the natives lived in thatch homes open to the soothing trade winds, the missionaries built airless clapboard houses with New England-style fireplaces. While the Polynesians swam and surfed frequently, the new arrivals, living near the world's finest beaches, stank from not bathing. In a region where the thermometer rarely drops much below seventy degrees, they wore long-sleeved woolens, ankle-length dresses and claw-hammer coats. At dinner they preferred salt pork to fresh beef, dried meat to fresh fish. They considered coconuts an abomination and were loath to eat bananas.

And yet the missionaries were a brave people, selfless and God-fearing. Their dangerous voyage from the Atlantic had brought them into a very alien land. Many would die from disease and overwork; most would never see their homeland again. Bigoted though they were, the Calvinists committed their lives to the Hawaiian people. They developed the Hawaiian alphabet, rendered Hawaiian into a written language and, of course, translated the Bible. Theirs was the first printing press west of the Rockies. They introduced Western medicine throughout the islands and created such an effective school system that, by the mid-19th century, 80 percent of the Hawaiian population was literate. Unlike almost all the other white people who came to Hawaii, they not only took from the islanders, they also gave.

But to a missionary, *giving* means ripping away everything repugnant to God and substituting it with Christianity. They would have to de-

---

MAUI CHIMES

All over the world, students of the steel guitar often begin their careers with a simple piece called "Maui Chimes." This melody, played in the key of A, is a standard in the repertoire of practically every well-known steel guitarist.

The first whaling ship arrived in Lahaina in 1819—the Balena *from Massachusetts.*

---

stroy Hawaiian culture in order to save it. Though instructed by their church elders not to meddle in island politics, the missionaries soon realized that heavenly wars had to be fought on earthly battlefields. Politics it would be. After all, wasn't government just another expression of God's bounty?

They allied with Kaahumanu and found it increasingly difficult to separate church from state. Kaahumanu converted to Christianity, while the missionaries became government advisers and helped pass laws protecting the sanctity of the Sabbath. Disgusting practices such as hula dancing were prohibited.

Politics can be a dangerous world for a man of the cloth. The missionaries were soon pitted against other foreigners who were quite willing to let the clerics sing hymns, but were adamantly opposed to permitting them a voice in government. Hawaii in the 1820s had become a favorite way station for the whaling fleet. As the sandalwood forests were destroyed, the island merchants began looking for other industries. By the 1840s, when over 500 ships a year anchored in Hawaiian ports, whaling had become the islands' economic lifeblood. More American ships visited Hawaii than any other port in the world. On Maui, the population soared to 35,000 and the economy boomed.

Like the missionaries, the whalers were Yankees, shipping out from bustling New England ports. But they were a different cut of Yankee: rough, crude, boisterous men who loved rum and music and thought a lot more of fornicating with island women than saving them. After the churchmen forced the passage of laws prohibiting prostitution, the sailors rioted along the waterfront and fired cannons at the mission homes. When the smoke cleared, the whalers still had their women. When the authorities tried to crack down on debauchery in Lahaina, a band of sailors from the whaling ship *Daniel*, brandishing a black flag, forced the local missionary to barricade himself in his house. Fearing for his life, he was finally rescued by a group of Hawaiians who drove the sailors back to their ship.

It was during the 1840s that Maui, led by a governor who placed money before mores, became a center for wild living. Lahaina, according to the missionaries, was the capital of sin, something of a seaside Sodom.

Religion simply could not compete with commerce, and other westerners were continuously stimulating more business in the islands. By the mid-19th century, as Hawaii adopted a parliamentary form of government, American and British fortune hunters were replacing missionaries as government advisers. It was a time when anyone, regardless of ability or morality, could travel to the islands and become a political powerhouse literally overnight. A consumptive American, fleeing the mainland for reasons of health, became chief justice of the Hawaiian Supreme Court while still in his twenties. Another lawyer, shadowed from the East Coast by a checkered past, became attorney general two weeks after arriving.

The situation was no different internationally. Hawaii was subject to the whims and terrors of gunboat diplomacy. The archipelago was solitary and exposed, and Western powers were beginning to eye it covetously. In 1843, a maverick British naval officer actually annexed Hawaii to the Crown, but the London government later countermanded his actions. Then, in the early 1850s, the threat of American annexation arose. Restless Californians, fresh from the gold fields and hungry for revolution, plotted unsuccessfully in Honolulu. Even the French periodically sent gunboats in to protect their small Catholic minority.

Finally, the three powers officially stated that they wanted to maintain Hawaii's national integrity. But independence seemed increasingly unlikely. European countries had already begun claiming other Pacific islands, and with the influx of Yankee missionaries and whalers, Hawaii was being steadily drawn into the American orbit.

THE SUGAR PLANTERS

There is an old Hawaiian saying that describes the 19th century: The missionaries came to do good, and they did very well. Actually the early evangelists, few of whom profited from their work, lived out only half the maxim. Their sons would give the saying its full meaning.

This second generation, quite willing to sacrifice glory for gain, fit neatly into the commercial society that had rendered their fathers irrelevant. They were shrewd, farsighted young Christians who had grown up in Hawaii and knew both the islands' pitfalls and potentials. They realized that the missionaries had never quite found Hawaii's pulse, and they watched uneasily as whaling became the lifeblood of the islands. Certainly it brought wealth, but whaling was too tenuous—there was always a threat that it might dry up entirely. A one-industry economy would never do; the mission boys wanted more. Agriculture was the obvious answer, and eventually they determined to bind their providence to a plant that grew wild in the islands—sugarcane.

In the years following the California gold rush of 1849, Maui's agricultural products were in particularly high demand. Prevailing winds persuaded many captains rounding Cape Horn en route to San Francisco to reprovision in Maui. Fresh fruits and vegetables, not to mention sugarcane plants, were plentiful and business for Upcountry farms expanded until the region earned the nickname *Nu Kaliponi*, or New California.

The first sugar plantation was actually started on Kauai in 1835 and on Maui in 1849, but not until the 1870s did the new industry blossom. By then, the Civil War had wreaked havoc with the whaling fleet, and a devastating winter in the Arctic whaling grounds practically destroyed it. The mission boys, who prophesied the storm, weathered it quite comfortably. They had already begun fomenting an agricultural revolution.

By the early 1860s, James Campbell had built Maui's first large sugar mill. Soon the center of island activity moved from Lahaina to the plantation town of Paia. A narrow-gauge railroad began operating between Kahului and Paia, and the island's population, which had been largely Polynesian and Caucasian, became increasingly Asian.

Agriculture, of course, means land, and in the 19th century practically all Hawaii's acreage was held by the king and the chiefs. So in 1850, the mission sons, together with other white entrepreneurs, pushed through the Great Mahele, one of the slickest real estate laws in history. Rationalizing that it would grant chiefs the liberty to sell land to Hawaiian commoners and white men, the mission sons established a Western system of private property.

The Hawaiians, who had shared their chiefs' lands communally for centuries, had absolutely no concept of deeds and leases. What resulted was the old $24-worth-of-beads story. The benevolent westerners wound up with the land, while the lucky Hawaiians got practically nothing. Large tracts were purchased for cases of whiskey; others went for the cost of a hollow promise. The entire island of Niihau, which is still owned by the same family, sold for $10,000. It was a bloodless coup, staged more than 40 years before the revolution that would topple Hawaii's monarchy. In a sense it made the 1893 uprising anticlimactic. By then Hawaii's future would already be determined: white interlopers would own four times as much land as Hawaiian commoners.

SPRECKELSVILLE

You have doubtless been losing sleep wondering how the old plantation town of Spreckelsville got its name. The moniker derives from Claus Spreckels, known locally as the Sugar King. This 19th-century robber baron combined business with politics, won the hearts and votes of Hawaii's leaders, and came to dominate the islands' sugar industry. Once, when the Hawaiian cabinet refused to grant him water rights, Spreckels lent a sum of money to King Kalakaua, who reciprocated by naming another cabinet. Spreckels also put His Majesty heavily into debt at the card table, forcing the legislature to retire the king's gambling debts with a special loan.

Hawaiian craftsmen produced the world's finest featherwork, weaving thousands of tiny feathers into golden cloaks and ceremonial helmets.

On Maui, James Makee established a plantation on the slopes of Hale-akala that sprawled across 1000 acres and produced up to 800 tons of sugar a year. His Rose Ranch, at Ulupalakua, became a lavish center of fashionable living. A piano and organ were imported to entertain those guests uninterested in the bowling alley and tennis court.

Following the Great Mahele, the mission boys, along with other businessmen like Makee, were ready to become sugar planters. The mana once again was passing into new hands. Obviously, there was money to be made in cane, a lot of it, and now that they had land, all they needed was labor. The Hawaiians would never do. Cook might have recognized them as industrious, hardworking people, but the sugar planters considered them shiftless. Disease was killing them off anyway, and the Hawaiians who survived seemed to lose the will to live. Many made appointments with death, stating that in a week they would die; seven days later they were dead.

Foreign labor was the only answer. In 1850, the Masters and Servants Act was passed, establishing an immigration board to import plantation workers. Cheap Asian labor would be brought over. It was a crucial decision, one that would ramify forever through Hawaiian history and change the very substance of island society. Between 1850 and 1930, 180,000 Japanese, 125,000 Filipinos, 50,000 Chinese and 20,000 Portuguese immigrated. They transformed Hawaii from a chain of Polynesian islands into one of the world's most varied and dynamic locales, a meeting place of East and West.

The Chinese were the first to come, arriving in 1852 and soon outnumbering the white population. Initially, with their long pigtails and unusual habits, the Chinese were a joke around the islands. They were poor people from southern China whose lives were directed by clan loyalty. They built schools and worked hard so that one day they could return to their native villages in glory. They were ambitious, industrious and—ultimately—successful.

Too successful, according to the sugar planters, who found it almost impossible to keep the coolies down on the farm. The Chinese came to Hawaii under labor contracts, which forced them to work for five years. After their indentureship, rather than reenlisting as the sugar bosses had planned, the Chinese moved to the city and became merchants. Worse yet, they married Hawaiian women and were assimilated into the society.

These coolies, the planters decided, were too uppity, too ready to fill social roles that were really the province of white men. So in the 1880s, they began importing Portuguese. But the Portuguese thought they already *were* white men, while any self-respecting American or Englishman of the time knew they weren't.

The Portuguese spelled trouble, and in 1886 the sugar planters turned to Japan, with its restricted land mass and burgeoning population. The new immigrants were peasants from Japan's southern islands, raised in an authoritarian, hierarchical culture in which the father was a family dictator and the family was strictly defined by its social status. Like the Chinese, they built schools to protect their heritage and dreamed of returning home someday; but unlike their Asian neighbors, they only married other Japanese. They sent home for "picture brides," worshipped their ancestors and Emperor and paid ultimate loyalty to Japan, not Hawaii.

The Japanese, it soon became evident, were too proud to work long hours for low pay. Plantation conditions were atrocious; workers were housed in hovels and frequently beaten. The Japanese simply did not adapt. Worst of all, they not only bitched, they organized, striking in 1909.

So in 1910, the sugar planters turned to the Philippines for labor. For two decades the Filipinos arrived, seeking their fortunes and leaving their wives behind. They worked not only with sugarcane but also with pineapples, which were becoming a big business in the 20th century. They were a boisterous, fun-loving people, hated by the immigrants who preceded them and used by the whites who hired them. The Filipinos were given the most menial jobs, the worst working conditions and the shoddiest housing. In time, another side of their character began to show—a despondency, a hopeless sense of their own plight, their inability to raise passage money back home. They became the untouchables of Hawaii.

The sugar industry on Maui, and throughout the islands, was dominated by a sugar refiner named Claus Spreckels, from San Francisco. Buying in to a Maui sugar plantation in 1877, he set his sights on the isthmus that separates Haleakala from the West Maui Mountains. Two other sugar planters, Samuel T. Alexander and Henry P. Baldwin, sons of missionaries, who founded Alexander & Baldwin, one of Hawaii's largest companies, were already digging a 17-mile-long irrigation ditch to their Haiku plantation.

Spreckels, also known as the "Sugar King," manipulated Hawaii's real monarch with bribes and loans into granting him invaluable water rights. Neither Baldwin nor Alexander were any match for "His Royal Saccharinity." By 1880, Maui began yielding the Sugar King's first crop.

REVOLUTIONARIES AND ROYALISTS

Sugar, by the late 19th century, was king. It had become the center of island economy, the principal fact of life for most islanders. Like the earlier whaling industry, it was drawing Hawaii ever closer to the American sphere. The sugar planters were selling the bulk of their crops in Califor-

The first president of Hawaii, Sanford Dole, was a missionary boy whose name eventually became synonymous with pineapples.

nia; having already signed several tariff treaties to protect their American market, they were eager to further strengthen mainland ties. Besides, many sugar planters were second-, third- and fourth-generation descendants of the New England missionaries; they had a natural affinity for the United States.

There was, however, one group that shared neither their love for sugar nor their ties to America. To the Hawaiian people, David Kalakaua was king, and America was the nemesis that had long threatened their independence. The whites might own the land, but the Hawaiians, through their monarch, still held substantial political power. During Kalakaua's rule in the 1870s and 1880s, anticolonialism was rampant.

The sugar planters were growing impatient. Kalakaua was proving very antagonistic; his nationalist drumbeating was becoming louder in their ears. How could the sugar merchants convince the United States to annex Hawaii when all these silly Hawaiian royalists were running around pretending to be the Pacific's answer to the British Isles? They had tolerated this long enough. The Hawaiians were obviously unfit to rule, and the planters soon joined with other businessmen to form a secret revolutionary organization. Backed by a force of well-armed followers, they pushed through the "Bayonet Constitution" of 1887, a self-serving document that weakened the king and strengthened the white landowners. If Hawaii was to remain a monarchy, it would have a Magna Carta.

But Hawaii would not be a monarchy long. Once revolution is in the air, it's often difficult to clear the smoke. By 1893, Kalakaua was dead and his sister, Liliuokalani, had succeeded to the throne. She was an audacious leader, proud of her heritage, quick to defend it and prone to let immediate passions carry her onto dangerous ground. At a time when she should have hung fire, she charged, proclaiming publicly that she would abrogate the new constitution and reestablish a strong monarchy. The revolutionaries had the excuse they needed. They struck in January, seized government buildings and, with four boatloads of American marines and the support of the American minister, secured Honolulu. Liliuokalani surrendered.

It was a highly illegal coup; legitimate government had been stolen from the Hawaiian people. But given an island chain as isolated and vulnerable as Hawaii, the revolutionaries reasoned, how much did it really matter? It would be weeks before word reached Washington of what a few Americans had done without official sanction, then several more months before a new American president, Grover Cleveland, de-

People often refer to Maui's racial mixes as a "chop suey" blend of humanity.

nounced the renegade action. By then the revolutionaries would already be forming a republic.

Not even revolution could rock Hawaii into the modern age. For years, an unstable monarchy had reigned; now an oligarchy composed of the revolution's leaders would rule. Officially, Hawaii was a democracy; in truth, the Chinese and Japanese were hindered from voting, and the Hawaiians were encouraged not to bother. Hawaii, reckoned its new leaders, was simply not ready for democracy.

More than ever before, the sugar planters, alias revolutionaries, held sway. By the early 20th century, they had linked their plantations into a cartel, the Big Five. It was a tidy monopoly composed of five companies that owned not only the sugar and pineapple industries, but also the docks, shipping companies and many of the stores, as well. Most of these holdings, happily, were the property of a few interlocking, intermarrying mission families—the Doles, Thurstons, Alexanders, Baldwins, Castles, Cookes and others—who had found heaven right here on earth. They golfed together and dined together, sent their daughters to Wellesley and their sons to Yale. All were proud of their roots, and as blindly paternalistic as their forefathers. It was their destiny to control Hawaii, and they made very certain, by refusing to sell land or provide services, that mainland firms did not gain a foothold in their domain.

What was good for the Big Five was good for Hawaii. Competition was obviously not good for Hawaii. Although the Chinese and Japanese were establishing successful businesses in Honolulu and some Chinese were even growing rich, they posed no immediate threat to the Big Five. And the Hawaiians had never been good at capitalism. By the early 20th century, they had become one of the world's most urbanized groups. But rather than competing with white businessmen in Honolulu, unemployed Hawaiians were forced to live in hovels and packing crates, cooking their poi on stoves fashioned from empty oil cans.

Political competition was also unhealthy. Hawaii was ruled by the Big Five, so naturally it should be run by the Republican Party. After all, the mission families were Republicans. Back on the mainland, the Democrats had always been cool to the sugar planters, and it was a Republican president, William McKinley, who eventually annexed Hawaii. The Republicans, quite simply, were good for business.

The Big Five set out very deliberately to overwhelm any political opposition. When the Hawaiians created a home-rule party around the turn of the century, the Big Five shrewdly co-opted it by running a beloved descendant of Hawaii's royal family as the Republican candidate. On the plantations they pitted one ethnic group against another to prevent the Asian workers from organizing. Then, when labor unions finally formed, the Big Five attacked them savagely. In 1924, police killed 16 strikers on Kauai. Fourteen years later, in an incident known as the "Hilo massacre," the police wounded 50 picketers.

The Big Five crushed the Democratic Party by intimidation. Polling booths were rigged. It was dangerous to vote Democratic—workers could lose their jobs, and if they were plantation workers, that meant losing their houses, as well. Conducting Democratic meetings on the plantations was about as easy as holding a hula dance in an old missionary church. The Democrats went underground.

Those were halcyon days for both the Big Five and the Republican Party. In 1900, only five percent of Hawaii's population was white. The rest comprised races that rarely benefitted from Republican policies. But for the next several decades, even during the Depression, the Big Five kept the Republicans in power.

While the New Deal swept the mainland, Hawaii clung to its colonial heritage. The islands were still a generation behind the rest of the United States—the Big Five preferred it that way. There was nothing like the status quo when you were already in power. Other factors that had long shaped Hawaii's history also played into the hands of the Big Five. The islands' vulnerability, which had always favored the rule of a small elite, permitted the Big Five to establish a formidable cartel. Hawaii's isolation, its distance from the mainland, helped protect their monopoly.

THE JAPANESE AND THE MODERN WORLD

All that ended on December 7, 1941. The Japanese bombers that attacked Pearl Harbor sent shock waves through Hawaii that are still rumbling today. World War II changed all the rules of the game, upsetting the conditions that had determined island history for centuries.

CREAMED ONIONS

Everyone knows about the shortages and rationing during World War II. But few have heard about the great Maui surplus. It seems that in May 1942, as local farmers were about to harvest a bumper crop of sweet Maui onions, a shipment of 900 tons of onions arrived on the island. The local populace responded with an innovative "Maui Onion Week," touting delights such as "creamed onions." Onion breath had become patriotic!

Ironically, no group in Hawaii would feel the shift more thoroughly than the Japanese. When the Emperor declared war on the United States, 160,000 Japanese-Americans were living in Hawaii, fully one-third of the islands' population. On the mainland, Japanese-Americans were rounded up and herded into relocation camps. But in Hawaii that was impossible; there were simply too many, and they comprised too large a part of the labor force.

Many were second-generation Japanese, *nisei*, who had been educated in American schools and assimilated into Western society. Unlike their immigrant parents, the *issei*, they felt few ties to Japan. Their loyalties lay with America and, when war broke out, they determined to prove it. They joined the U.S. armed forces and formed a regiment, the 442nd, which became the most frequently decorated outfit of the war. The Japanese were heroes, and when the war ended many heroes came home to the United States and ran for political office. Men like Dwight Eisenhower, Daniel Inouye, John Kennedy and Spark Matsunaga began winning elections.

By the time the 442nd returned to the home front, Hawaii was changing dramatically. The Democrats were coming to power. Leftist labor unions won crucial strikes in 1941 and 1946. Jack Burns, an ex-cop who dressed in tattered clothes and drove around Honolulu in a beat-up car, was creating a new Democratic coalition.

Burns, who would eventually become governor, recognized the potential power of Hawaii's ethnic groups. Money was flowing into the islands—first military expenditures and then tourist dollars—and non-whites were rapidly becoming a new middle class. The Filipinos still constituted a large part of the plantation workforce, and the Hawaiians remained disenchanted, but the Japanese and Chinese were moving up fast. Together they comprised a majority of Hawaii's voters.

Burns organized them, creating a multiracial movement and thrusting the Japanese forward as candidates. By 1954, the Democrats controlled the legislature, with the Japanese filling one out of every two seats in the capital. Then, when Hawaii attained statehood five years later, the voters elected the first Japanese ever to serve in Congress. Today one of the state's U.S. senators and a congressman are Japanese. On every level of government, from municipal to federal, the Japanese predominate. They

---

TORA! TORA! TORA!

Although Oahu was devastated by the Japanese attack on Pearl Harbor, Maui suffered but a single casualty. A week after the Pacific war began, the Maui Pineapple Company was hit by a pair of Japanese submarine shells. Total damage: $700.

have arrived. The *mana*, that legendary power coveted by the Hawaiian chiefs and then lost to the sugar barons, has passed once again—to a people who came as immigrant farm-workers and stayed to become the leaders of the 50th state.

The Japanese and the Democrats were on the move, but in the period from World War II until the present day, everything was in motion. Hawaii was in upheaval. Jet travel and a population boom shattered the islands' solitude. While in 1939 about 500 people flew to Hawaii, now more than six million land every year. The military population escalated as Oahu became a key base not only during World War II but throughout the Cold War and the Vietnam War, as well. Hawaii's overall population exploded from about a half-million just after World War II to over one million at the present time.

No longer did the islands lag behind the mainland; they rapidly acquired the dubious quality of modernity. Hawaii became America's 50th state in 1959, Honolulu grew into a bustling highrise city, and condominiums mushroomed along Maui's beaches. In 1961, the Kaanapali area of Maui became the first resort complex to be built on a neighbor island.

Outside investors swallowed up two of the Big Five corporations, and several partners in the old monopoly began conducting most of their business outside Hawaii. Everything became too big and moved too fast for Hawaii to be entirely vulnerable to a small interest group. Now, like the rest of the world, it would be prey to multi-national corporations.

By the 1980s, it would also be of significant interest to investors from Japan. In a few short years they succeeded in buying up a majority of the state's luxury resorts, including every major beachfront hotel in Waikiki and a number of resorts on Maui, sending real estate prices into an upward spiral that did not level off until the early 1990s. Hawaii had arrived; it was fully a part of the modern world. An island chain that had slept for centuries had been rudely awakened by the forces of change.

Culture

Hawaii, according to Polynesian legend, was discovered by Hawaii-loa, an adventurous sailor who often disappeared on long fishing trips. On one voyage, urged along by his navigator, Hawaii-loa sailed toward the planet Jupiter. He crossed the "many-colored ocean," passed over the "deep-colored sea," and eventually came upon "flaming Hawaii," a mountainous island chain that spewed smoke and lava.

History is less romantic. The Polynesians who found Hawaii were probably driven from their home islands by war or some similar calamity. They traveled in groups, not as lone rangers, and shared their canoes with dogs, pigs and chickens, with which they planned to stock new lands. Agricultural plants such as coconuts, yams, taro, sugarcane, bananas and breadfruit were also stowed on board.

Most important, they transported their culture, an intricate system of beliefs and practices developed in the South Seas. After undergoing the stresses and demands of pioneer life, this traditional lifestyle was transformed into a new and uniquely Hawaiian culture.

It was based on a caste system that placed the *alii* or chiefs at the top and the slaves, *kauwas*, on the bottom. Between these two groups were the priests, *kahunas*, and the common people, or *makaainanas*. The chiefs, much like feudal lords, controlled all the land and collected taxes from the commoners who farmed it. Each island was divided like a pie into wedge-shaped plots, *ahupuaas*, which extended from the ocean to the mountain peaks. In that way, every chief's domain contained fishing spots, village sites, arable valleys and everything else necessary for the survival of his subjects.

Life centered around the *kapu*, a complex group of regulations that dictated what was sacred or profane. For example, women were not permitted to eat pork or bananas; commoners had to prostrate themselves in the presence of a chief. These strictures were vital to Hawaiian religion; *kapu* breakers were directly violating the will of the gods and could be executed for their actions. And there were a lot of gods to watch out for, many quite vindictive. The four central gods were *Kane*, the creator; *Lono*, the god of agriculture; *Ku*, the war god; and *Kanaloa*, lord of the underworld. They had been born from the sky father and earth mother, and had in turn created many lesser gods and demigods who controlled various aspects of nature.

It was, in the uncompromising terminology of the West, a stone-age civilization. Though the Hawaiians lacked metal tools, the wheel and a writing system, they managed to include within their short inventory of cultural goods everything necessary to sustain a large population on a chain of small islands. They fashioned fish nets from coconut fibers, made hooks out of bone, shell and ivory, and raised fish in rock-bound ponds. The men used irrigation in their farming. The women made clothing by pounding mulberry bark into a soft cloth called tapa, dyeing elaborate patterns into the fabric. They built peak-roofed thatch huts from native *pili* grass and *lauhala* leaves. The men fought wars with spears, slings, clubs and daggers! The women used mortars and pestles to pound the roots of the taro plant into *poi*, the islanders' staple food.

The West labeled these early Hawaiians "noble savages." Actually, they often lacked nobility. The Hawaiians were cannibals who sometimes practiced human sacrifice and often used human bait to fish for sharks. They constantly warred among themselves and would mercilessly pursue a retreating army, murdering as many of the vanquished soldiers as possible.

But they weren't savages either. The Hawaiians developed a rich oral tradition of genealogical chants and created beautiful lilting songs to accompany their hula dancing. The Hawaiians helped develop the sport of surfing. They also swam, boxed, bowled and devised an intriguing game called *konane*, a cross between checkers and the Japanese game of *go*. They built hiking trails from coral and lava, and created an elemental art form in the images—petroglyphs—that they carved into rocks along the trails.

They also achieved something far more outstanding than their varied arts and crafts, something which the West, with its awesome knowledge and advanced technology, has never duplicated. The Hawaiians on Maui and other islands created a balance with nature. They practiced conservation, establishing closed seasons on certain fish species and carefully guarding their plant and animal resources. They led a simple life, without the complexities the outside world would eventually thrust upon them. It was a good life: food was plentiful, people were healthy, and the population increased. For a thousand years, the Hawaiians lived in delicate harmony with the elements. It wasn't until the West entered the realm, transforming everything, that the fragile balance was destroyed. But that is another story entirely.

The People

Because of its unique history and isolated geography, Hawaii is truly a cultural melting pot. It's one of the few states in the union in which white people are a minority group. Whites, or haoles as they're called in the islands, comprise only about 33 percent of Hawaii's 1.1 million population. Japanese constitute 22 percent, Filipinos 15 percent, Hawaiians and part-Hawaiians account for 12 percent, Chinese about six percent and other racial groups three percent. The population of Maui is almost 100,000 and the ethnic mix is similar to that in the rest of the islands.

It's a very young, vital society. More than half the community is under thirty-five and over one-quarter of the people were born of racially mixed parents. Three out of every four residents live on the island of Oahu, and almost half of those live in the city of Honolulu.

One trait characterizing many of these people is Hawaii's famous spirit of *aloha*, a genuine friendliness, an openness to strangers, a willingness to give freely. Undoubtedly, it is one of the finest qualities any people has ever demonstrated. *Aloha* originated with the Polynesians and played an important role in ancient Hawaiian civilization. When Western colonialists arrived, however, they viewed it not as a Hawaiian form of graciousness, but rather as the naivete of a primitive culture. They turned *aloha* into a tool for exploiting the Hawaiians, taking practically everything they owned.

Today, unfortunately, the descendants of the colonialists are being repaid in kind. The *aloha* spirit is still present in the islands, but another social force has arisen—racial hatred. There is growing resentment toward white people and other mainlanders in Hawaii.

Sometimes this hatred spills into ripoffs and violence. Therefore, mainland visitors must be very careful, particularly when traveling in heavily touristed areas. Try not to leave items in your car; if you absolutely must, lock them in the trunk. Don't leave valuable gear unattended in a campsite. And try not to antagonize the islands' young people.

It's exciting to meet folks, and I highly recommend that you mix with local residents, but do it with forethought and consideration. A lot of locals are eager to make new acquaintances; others can be extremely hostile. So choose the situation. If a local group looks bent on trouble, mind your own business. They don't need you, and you don't need them. For most encounters, I'd follow this general rule—be friendly, but be careful.

The Cuisine

Nowhere is the influence of Hawaii's melting pot population stronger than in the kitchen. While on Maui, you'll probably eat not only with a fork, but with chopsticks and fingers, as well. You'll sample a wonder-

---

LUAUS

Everyone leaves the diet behind when signing up for a night of music and dance at one of Maui's fabled luaus. This Hawaiian tradition is maintained by community organizations, who advertise the events in the newspaper, and, in a manner of speaking, by major resorts, who sponsor splashy shows. Whether you decide to take in the local color at a neighborhood feast or check out the heavily commercialized "luaus" at the big hotels, be sure to bring a healthy appetite.

*The **Old Lahaina Luau** (505 Front Street, Lahaina; 667-1998) is a small event, staged on the waterfront in a historic region favored by Hawaiian monarchs. Cast members arrive by outrigger canoe and offer a succession of entertaining Polynesian dances. The hula instruction is first rate, as is the lomilomi salmon. Daily.*

*At the torchlit **Royal Lahaina Luau** (2780 Kekaa Drive, Kaanapali; 661-3611) hula lessons, corny jokes and Tahitian dance are all part of the show. Performers also re-create famed Hawaiian legends at this oceanfront show. Open bar. Nightly.*

*Ranging from New Zealand to Hawaii, **Drums of the Pacific Luau** (200 Nohea Kai Drive, Kaanapali; 661-1234) blends traditional luau events such as the imu ceremony with fire dances and Tahitian performances. This glitzy program, staged in an amphitheater at the Hyatt Regency Maui, is one of the island's best examples of a hotel luau. Monday, Tuesday, Wednesday, Friday and Saturday.*

*The **Marriott Luau** (100 Nohea Kai Drive, Kaanapali; 667-8226) is the place to pig out on pig (not to mention teriyaki beef, sweet-and-sour chicken and*

fully varied cuisine. In addition to standard American fare, hundreds of restaurants serve Hawaiian, Japanese, Chinese, Korean, Portuguese and Filipino dishes. There are also fresh fruits aplenty—pineapples, papayas, mangoes, bananas and tangerines—plus native fish such as mahimahi, marlin and snapper.

The prime Hawaiian dish is *poi*, made from crushed taro root and served as a pasty purple liquid. It's pretty bland fare, but it does make a good side dish with roast pork or tripe stew. You should also try *laulau*, a combination of fish, pork and taro leaves wrapped in a *ti* leaf and steamed. And don't neglect to taste baked ulu (breadfruit) and opihi (limpets).

Among the other Hawaiian culinary traditions are *kalua* pig, a shredded pork dish baked in an *imu*; *lomilomi* salmon, which is salted and mixed with onions and tomatoes; and chicken *laulau*, prepared in taro leaves and coconut milk.

A good way to try all these dishes at one sitting is to attend a *luau*. I've always found the tourist *luaus* too commercial, but you might watch the newspapers for one of the special *luaus* sponsored by civic organizations.

Japanese dishes include sushi, sukiyaki, teriyaki and tempura, plus an island favorite—sashimi, or raw fish. On most any menu, including

---

mahimahi). Where else can you learn traditional Hawaiian crafts and games while enjoying Polynesian performers? Tuesday through Sunday.

The **Wailea Sunset Luau** *(3550 Wailea Alanui Drive, Wailea; 879-4900) offers everything from the classic unearthing of a pig from an underground oven (*imu*), to Tahitian and Fijian performances to a Samoan fire-knife dance. This Stouffer Wailea Beach Resort event is famous for its dessert bar (especially the pineapple upside-down cake). Monday and Thursday.*

Another popular event, **Wailea's Finest Luau** *(3700 Wailea Alanui Drive, Wailea; 879-1922) at the Maui Inter-Continental Resort, is set in an oceanfront garden. It's a Polynesian spectacular starring Paradyse and Ka Poe O Hawaii. Don't miss the macadamia nut pie. Tuesday, Thursday and Friday.*

Classic and modern hula are highlighted at the **Grand Ohana Luau** *(3850 Wailea Alanui Drive, Wailea; 875-1234), which provides an entertaining glimpse into Polynesian heritage. Buffet specialties at this Grand Wailea Resort and Spa presentation include kalua pig, poi, onaga and teriyaki beef. Wednesday.*

The Hotel Hana Maui's **Hamoa Beach Luau** *(248-8211) combines the amenities of a major resort with a warm community atmosphere. Staged at a site James Michener called "the most perfect crescent beach in the Pacific," the event includes local families and a number of the hotel's employees. Tuesday.*

McDonald's, you'll find *saimin*, a noodle soup filled with meat, vegetables and *kamaboko* (fishcake).

You can count on the Koreans for *kim chi*, a spicy salad of pickled cabbage, and *kun koki*, barbecued meat prepared with soy and sesame oil. The Portuguese serve up some delicious sweets including *malasadas* (donuts minus the holes) and *pao doce*, or sweet bread. For Filipino fare, I recommend *adobo*, a pork or chicken dish spiced with garlic and vinegar, and *pochero*, a meat entrée cooked with bananas and several vegetables. In addition to a host of dinner dishes, the Chinese have contributed some less common treats such as *manapua* (a steamed bun filled with barbecued pork) and oxtail soup. They also introduced crack seed to the islands. Made from dried and preserved fruit, it provides a treat as sweet as candy.

As the Hawaiians say, *"Hele mai ai."* Come and eat!

The Language

The language common to all Hawaii is English, but because of its diverse cultural heritage, the archipelago also supports several other tongues. Foremost among these are Hawaiian and pidgin.

Hawaiian, closely related to other Polynesian languages, is one of the most fluid and melodious languages in the world. It's composed of only 12 letters: five vowels—*a, e, i, o, u* and seven consonants—*h, k, l, m, n, p, w.*

At first glance, the language appears formidable: how the hell do you pronounce *humuhumunukunukuapuaa*? But actually it's quite simple. After you've mastered a few rules of pronunciation, you can take on any word in the language.

The first thing to remember is that every syllable ends with a vowel, and the next to last syllable receives the accent.

The next rule to keep in mind is that all the letters in Hawaiian are pronounced. Consonants are pronounced the same as in English (except for the *w*, which is pronounced as a *v* when it introduces the last syllable of a word—as in *ewa* or *awa*. Vowels are pronounced the same as in Latin or Spanish: *a* as in *among*, *e* as in *they*, *i* as in *machine*, *o* as in *no* and *u* as in *too*. Hawaiian has four vowel combinations or diphthongs: *au*, pronounced *ow*, *ae* and *ai*, which sound like *eye*, and *ei*, pronounced *ay*.

By now, you're probably wondering what I could possibly have meant when I said Hawaiian was simple. I think the glossary that follows will simplify everything while helping you pronounce common words and place names. Just go through the list, starting with words like *aloha* and *luau* that you already know. After you've practiced pronouncing familiar words, the rules will become second nature; you'll practically be a *kamaaina*.

Just when you start to speak with a swagger, cocky about having learned a new language, some young Hawaiian will start talking at you in a tongue that breaks all the rules you've so carefully mastered. That's pidgin. It started in the 19th century as a lingua franca among Hawaii's many races. Pidgin speakers mix English and Hawaiian with several other tongues to produce a spicy creole. It's a fascinating language with its own vocabulary, a unique syntax and a rising inflection that's hard to mimic.

Pidgin is definitely the hip way to talk in Hawaii. A lot of young Hawaiians use it among themselves as a private language. At times they may start talking pidgin to you, acting as though they don't speak English; then if they decide you're okay, they'll break into English. When that happens, you be one *da kine brah*.

So *brah*, I take *da kine* pidgin words, put 'em together with Hawaiian, make one big list. Savvy?

aa (**ah**-ah) - a type of rough lava

ae (eye) - yes

aikane (eye-**kah**-nay) - friend

akamai (ah-**kah**-my) - wise

alii (ah-**lee**-ee) - chief

aloha (ah-**lo**-ha) - hello; greetings; love

aole (ah-**oh**-lay) - no

auwe (ow-**way**) - ouch!

brah (bra) - friend; brother; bro'

bumby (**bum**-bye) - after awhile; by and by

dah makule guys (da mah-**kuh**-lay guys) - senior citizens

da kine (da kyne) - whatdyacallit; thingamajig; that way

diamondhead - in an easterly direction

duh uddah time (duh **uh**-duh time) - once before

ewa (**eh**-vah) - in a westerly direction

hale (**hah**-lay) - house

haole (**how**-lee) - Caucasian; white person

hapa (**hah**-pa) - half

hapa-haole (**hah**-pa **how**-lee) - half-Caucasian

heiau (hey-ee-**ow**) - temple

hele on (**hey**-lay own) - hip; with it

holo holo (**ho**-low **ho**-low) - to visit

howzit? (hows-it) - how you doing? what's happening?

hukilau (**who**-key-lau) - community fishing party

hula (**who**-la) - Hawaiian dance

imu (**ee**-moo) - underground oven

ipo (**ee**-po) - sweetheart

jag up (jag up) - drunk

kahuna (kah-**who**-nah) - priest

kai (kye) - ocean

kaka-roach (**kah**-kah roach) - ripoff; theft

kamaaina (kah-mah-**eye**-nah) - a longtime island resident *kane* (**kah**-nay) – man

kapu (**kah**-poo) – taboo; forbidden

kaukau (cow-cow) – food

keiki (**kay**-key) – child

kiawe (key-**ah**-vay) – mesquite tree

kokua (ko-**coo**-ah) – help

kona winds (**ko**-nah winds) – winds that blow against the trades

lanai (lah-**nye**) – porch; also island name

lauhala (lau-**hah**-lah) or *hala* (**hah**-lah) – a tree whose leaves are used
   in weaving

lei (lay) – flower garland

lolo (low-low) – stupid

lomilomi (**low**-me-**low**-me) – massage; also raw salmon

luau (**loo**-ow) – feast

mahalo (mah-**hah**-low) – thank you

mahalo nui loa (mah-**hah**-low **new**-ee **low**-ah) – thank you very much

mahu (**mah**-who) – gay; homosexual

makai (mah-**kye**) – toward the sea

malihini (mah-lee-**hee**-nee) – newcomer; stranger

mauka (**mau**-kah) – toward the mountains

nani (**nah**-nee) – beautiful

ohana (oh-**hah**-nah) – family

okole (oh-**ko**-lay) – rear; ass

okolemaluna (oh-ko-lay-mah-**loo**-nah) – a toast: bottoms up!

ono (**oh**-no) – tastes good

pahoehoe (pah-**hoy**-hoy) – ropy lava

pakalolo (pah-kah-**low**-low) – marijuana

pakiki head (pah-**key**-key head) – stubborn

pali (**pah**-lee) – cliff

paniolo (pah-nee-**oh**-low) – cowboy

pau (pow) – finished; done

pilikia (pee-lee-**key**-ah) – trouble

puka (**poo**-kah) – hole

pupus (**poo**-poos) – hors d'oeuvres

shaka (**shah**-kah) – great; perfect

swell head – angry

tapa (**tap**-ah) – tree bark which is used as a fabric

wahine (wah-**hee**-nay) – woman

wikiwiki (**wee**-key-**wee**-key) – quickly; in a hurry

you get stink ear – you don't listen well

Music and Dance

MUSIC

Music has long been an integral part of Hawaiian life. Most families keep musical instruments in their homes, gathering to play at impromptu living-room or backyard jam sessions. Hawaiian folk tunes are passed down from generation to generation. In the earliest days, it was the sound of rhythm instruments and chants that filled the air. Drums were fashioned from hollowed-out gourds, coconut shells and breadfruit logs, then covered with sharkskin. Gourds and coconuts, adorned with tapa cloth and feathers, were also filled with shells or pebbles to produce a rattling sound. Other instruments included the nose flute, a piece of bamboo similar to a mouth flute, but played by exhaling through the nostril; the bamboo organ; and *puili*, pieces of bamboo split into strips, which were struck rhythmically against the body.

Western musical scales and instruments were introduced by explorers and missionaries. As ancient Hawaiian music involved a completely different musical system, Hawaiians had to completely re-adapt. Actually, western music caught on quickly, and the hymns brought by missionaries fostered a popular musical style—the *himeni* or Hawaiian church music.

Strangely enough, a Prussian bandmaster named Henry Berger had a major influence on contemporary Hawaiian music. Brought over by King Kalakaua to lead the Royal Hawaiian Band, Berger helped Hawaiians make the transition to western instruments.

Hawaii has been the birthplace of several different musical instruments and styles. The ukulele, modeled on a Portuguese guitar, quickly became the most popular Hawaiian instrument. Its small size made it easy to carry, and with just four strings, it was simple to play. During the early 1900s, the steel guitar was exported to the mainland. Common in country-and-western music today, it was invented by a young man who experimented by sliding a steel bar across guitar strings.

The slack-key style of guitar playing also comes from Hawaii. In tuning, the six strings are loosened and then played in a variety of ways, from plucking or slapping the strings to sliding along them. A number of different tunings exist, and many have been passed down through families for generations.

During the late 19th century, "*hapa*-haole" songs became the rage. The ukelele was instrumental in contributing to this Hawaiian fad. Written primarily in English with pseudo-Hawaiian themes, songs like "Tiny Bubbles" and "Lovely Hula Hands" were later introduced to the world via Hollywood.

The Hawaiian craze continued on the mainland with radio and television shows such as "Hawaii Calls" and "The Harry Owens Show." In

Tune in to KPOA-FM 93.5 and 107.3 for Hawaiian music (after 8 p.m. the sounds are jazz).

the 1950s, little mainland girls donned plastic hula skirts and danced along with Hilo Hattie and Ray Kinney.

It was not until the 1970s that both the hula and music of old Hawaii made a comeback. Groups such as the Sons of Hawaii and the Makaha Sons of Niihau, along with Auntie Genoa Keawe and the late Gabby Pahinui, became popular. Before long, a new form of Hawaiian music was being heard, a combination of ancient chants and contemporary sounds, performed by such islanders as Cecelio and Kapono, Kalapana, Olomana, the Beamer Brothers, Karen Keawehawaii, the Peter Moon Band and the Brothers Cazimero.

Today many of these groups, along with other notables such as the Kaau Crater Boys, Palani Vaughn, Brother Nolan, Ohta San, Willie K and Butch Helemano, bring both innovation to the Hawaiian music scene and contribute to the preservation of an ancient tradition.

HULA

Along with palm trees, the hula—swaying hips, grass skirts, colorful leis—is linked forever in people's minds with the Hawaiian Islands. This western idea of hula is very different from what the dance has traditionally meant to native Hawaiians.

Hula is an old dance form, its origin shrouded in mystery. The ancient hula, *kahiko*, was more concerned with religion and spirituality than entertainment. Originally performed only by men, it was used in rituals to communicate with a deity—a connection to nature and the gods. Accompanied by drums and chants, *kahiko* expressed the islands' culture, mythology and history in hand and body movements. It later evolved from a strictly religious rite to a method of communicating stories and legends. Over the years, women were allowed to study the rituals and eventually became the primary dancers.

When westerners arrived, the *kahiko* hula began another transformation. Explorers and sailors were more interested in its erotic element, ignoring the cultural significance. Missionaries simply found it scandalous and set out to destroy the tradition. They dressed Hawaiians in western garb and outlawed the *kahiko* hula.

The hula tradition was resurrected by King David Kalakaua. Known by the moniker "Merrie Monarch," Kalakaua loved music and dance. For his coronation in 1883, he called together the kingdom's best dancers to perform the chants and hulas once again. He was also instrumental in the development of the contemporary hula, the *auwana* hula, which added new steps and movements and was accompanied by ukeleles and guitars rather than drums.

By the 1920s, modern hula had been popularized by Hollywood, westernized and introduced as kitschy tropicana. Real grass skirts gave way to cellophane versions, plastic leis replaced fragrant island garlands, and exaggerated gyrations supplanted the hypnotic movements of the traditional dance.

Fortunately, with the resurgence of Hawaiian pride in recent decades, Polynesian culture has been reclaimed and *kahiko* hula and chants have made a welcome comeback.

FOUR

Lahaina

Maui's top tourist destination is a waterfront enclave that stretches for over two miles along a natural harbor, but measures only a couple of blocks deep. Simultaneously chic and funky, Lahaina has gained an international reputation for its art galleries, falsefront stores and waterfront restaurants.

It also happens to be one of Hawaii's most historic towns. A royal seat since the 16th century, Lahaina was long a playground for the alii. The royal surfing grounds lay just south of today's town center, and in 1802, Kamehameha I established his headquarters here, taking up residence in the Brick Palace, the first Western-style building in Hawaii.

It was in Lahaina that the first high school and first printing press west of the Rockies were established in 1831. From Lahaina, Kamehameha III promulgated Hawaii's first constitution in 1840, and established a legislative body that met in town until the capital was eventually moved to Honolulu.

During the 1820s, this quaint port also became a vital watering place for whaling ships and evolved into the whaling capital of the world. At its peak in the mid-1840s, the whaling trade brought over 400 ships a year into the harbor.

To the raffish sailors who favored it for its superb anchorage, grog shops and uninhibited women, Lahaina was heaven itself. To the stiff-collared missionaries who arrived in 1823, the town was a hellhole—a place of sin, abomination and vile degradation. Some of Lahaina's most colorful history was written when the Congregationalists prevented naked women from swimming out to meet the whalers. Their belligerent brethren anchored in the harbor replied by cannonballing mission homes and rioting along the waterfront.

The town declined with the loss of the whaling trade in the 1860s, and was transformed into a quiet sugar plantation town, serving the Pioneer Sugar Mill that opened during the same decade. Not until developers began building resorts in nearby Kaanapali a century later did it fully revive. During the 1960s, Lahaina was designated a national historic landmark and restoration of many important sites was begun. By the 1970s, the place was a gathering spot not only for the jet set but the ultra hip as well. Clubs like the Blue Max made Lahaina a hot nightspot where famous musicians came to vacation and jam.

Today the town retains much of its old charm in the ramshackle storefronts that line the water along Front Street. Most points of interest lie within a half-mile of the old sea wall that protects this narrow thoroughfare from the ocean, so the best way to explore the town is on foot.

Start at **Lahaina Harbor** (Wharf Street) and take a stroll along the docks. In addition to tour boats, pleasure craft from around the world put in here or cast anchor in the Lahaina Roads just offshore. During the heyday of the whaling industry in the 1840s, the Auau Channel between Lahaina and Lanai was a forest of masts.

Carthaginian II (661-8527; admission), the steel-hulled brig at dock's end, preserves those days in a shipboard museum. Actually a turn-of-the-century brig that was converted into a replica of an old square-rigged sailing ship, this floating display case features videotapes on whales and intriguing artifacts from days of yore.

Across Wharf Street sits the **Pioneer Inn** (661-3636), a rambling hostelry built in 1901. With its second-story veranda and landscaped garden, this aging woodframe hotel is a great place to bend an elbow and breathe in the salt air.

Just north of here a Hawaii Visitors Bureau sign points out the chair-shaped **Hauola Stone**, a source of healing power for ancient Hawaiians, who sat in the natural formation and let the waves wash over them.

There is nothing left of the **Brick Palace** (just inshore from the Hauola Stone), the two-story structure commissioned in 1798 by Kamehameha I. Built by an English convict, the palace was used by the king in 1802 and 1803 (although some say he preferred to stay in his grass shack next door). Today the original foundation has been outlined with brick paving.

To the south, a 120-year-old **banyan tree** (Front and Hotel streets), among the oldest and largest in the islands, extends its rooting branches across almost an entire acre. Planted in 1873 to mark the advent of Protestant missionaries in Maui 50 years earlier, this shady canopy is a resting place for tourists and mynah birds alike.

The sprawling giant presses right to the **Old Courthouse** door. Built in 1859 from the remains of the palace of King Kamehameha III, the building was fashioned from coral blocks. The **Old Jail** in the basement now incongruously houses **The Lahaina Art Society** (661-0111), a

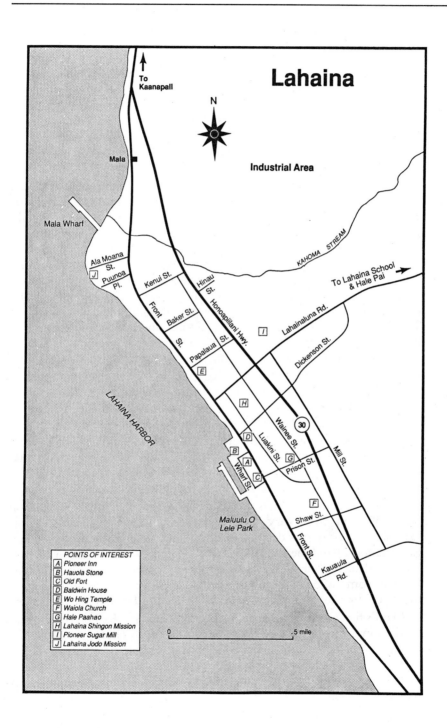

Lahaina

To
Kaanapali

N

Mala

Industrial Area

Mala Wharf

Ala Moana St.
J
Puunoa Pl.

Kenui St.

Hinau St.

KAHOMA STREAM

To Lahaina School
& Hale Pai

Front St.

Baker St.

Honoapiliani Hwy.

Lahainaluna Rd.

I

Papalaua St.

Dickenson St.

E

H

Wainee St.

30

D

Luakini St.

B

A

G

Mill St.

Wharf St.

C

Prison St.

F

LAHAINA HARBOR

Maluulu O
Lele Park

Shaw St.

Front St.

Kauaula Rd.

POINTS OF INTEREST
A Pioneer Inn
B Hauola Stone
C Old Fort
D Baldwin House
E Wo Hing Temple
F Waiola Church
G Hale Paahao
H Lahaina Shingon Mission
I Pioneer Sugar Mill
J Lahaina Jodo Mission

0 _____ .5 mile

Approximately 55 acres of Lahaina have been designated as a historic district.

---

nonprofit association of local artists. Exhibits at the gallery here are rotating collections of member artists.

Those stone ruins on either side of the courthouse are the remains of the **Old Fort**, built during the 1830s to protect Lahaina from the sins and cannonballs of lawless sailors. The original structure was torn down two decades later to build a jail, but during its heyday the fortress guarded the waterfront with 47 cannons.

Across Front Street you'll find the **Baldwin Home** (661-3262; admission), Lahaina's oldest building. Constructed of coral and stone in the early 1830s, the place sheltered the family of Reverend Dwight Baldwin, a medical missionary. Today the house contains period pieces and family heirlooms, including some of the good doctor's rather fiendish-looking medical implements. Beneath the hand-hewn ceiling beams rest the Baldwin's Steinway piano; the dining room includes the family's china, a fragile cargo that made the voyage around Cape Horn; and in the master bedroom stands a four-poster bed fashioned from native *koa*. The **Master's Reading Room** next door, an 1834 storehouse and library, is home to the local historical society and not open to the public.

The **Wo Hing Temple** (858 Front Street; 661-3262; admission), a Chinese gathering place that dates to 1912, has been lovingly restored. While the temple has been converted into a small museum, the old cookhouse adjacent is used to show films of the islands made by Thomas Edison in 1898 and 1906 during the early days of motion pictures.

The **Holy Innocents Episcopal Church** (561 Front Street; 661-4202) is a small structure dating from 1927. Very simple in design, the sanctuary is filled with beautiful paintings. The Hawaiian madonna on the altar and the tropical themes of the paintings are noteworthy features.

Several other historic spots lie along Wainee Street, which parallels Front Street. **Waiola Cemetery**, with its overgrown lawn and eroded tombstones, contains graves dating to 1829. Queen Keopuolani, the wife of Kamehameha I and the mother of Hawaii's next two kings, is buried here. So is her daughter, Princess Nahienaena, and Governor Hoapali, who ruled Hawaii from 1823 to 1840. Surrounded by blossoming plumeria trees, there are also the graves of early missionaries and Hawaiian commoners.

Maui's first Christian services were performed in 1823 on the grounds of **Waiola Church** (661-4349) next door. Today's chapel, built in 1953, occupies the spot where Wainee Church was constructed in 1832. The earlier structure, Hawaii's first stone church, seated 3000 parishioners and played a vital role in the conversion of the local population to Christianity and western ways.

A little farther north on Wainee Street sits the **Hongwanjii Temple** with its three distinctive turrets. The building dates from 1927, but the Buddhist Hongwanjii sect has been meeting at this site since 1910. It is currently the place of worship for Lahaina's main Buddhist congregation.

Down the street rise the menacing walls of old **Hale Paahao** (Prison and Wainee streets), a prison built by convicts in 1854 and used to house rowdy sailors as well as more hardened types. The coral blocks used to build this local hoosegow were taken from the Old Fort on Front Street.

Just north of the jail along Wainee Street sits the **Episcopal Cemetery** and **Hale Aloha**. Walter Murray Gibson, a controversial figure in 19th-century Hawaii politics who eventually became an adviser to King David Kalakaua, is buried here. Hale Aloha, completed in 1858 and restored several years ago, served as a church meetinghouse.

Nearby **Maria Lanakila Church** (Wainee and Dickenson streets), built in 1928 to replace a 19th-century chapel, is a lovely white-washed building with interior pillars. Adjacent is the **Seamen's Cemetery**, a poorly maintained ground where early sailors were laid to rest.

The **Lahaina Shingon Mission** (682 Luakini Street between Hale and Prison streets; 661-0466), a simple plantation-era structure with an ornately gilded altar, was built in 1902 by a Japanese monk and his followers. It now represents another gathering place for Maui's Buddhists.

The proverbial kids-from-eight-to-eighty set will love the **Sugar Cane Train** (661-0089; admission), a reconstructed 1890-era steam train. Operating around the West Maui resort area, the Lahaina-Kaanapali & Pacific Railroad engine and open passenger cars chug along a six-mile route midway between the mountains and ocean. Various package tours are available with the train rides, including a ride on a glass bottom boat in Lahaina, admission to three of Lahaina's museums, and a viewing of the film Hawaii: Islands of the Gods, shown on the 180-degree screen at the Omni Theatre. The main station is off Hinau Street in Lahaina.

Oceanic adventurers should take an opportunity to stop in at **Atlantis Submarines** (505 Front Street, in the Pioneer Inn; 667-2224) and reserve an underwater tour. The voyage takes you aboard a 46-passenger submersible down to depths of 150 feet. En route you may see close-up

---

ROYAL HAWAIIAN HOLIDAYS

Although the Hawaiian capital moved to Honolulu in 1850, Lahaina remained a favorite vacation spot for several kings, including Kamehameha III, IV and V, and Queen Liliuokalani. All had second homes in the area and returned often to indulge in those favorite Hawaiian pastimes, rest and relaxation.

The oldest American school west of the Rockies is Lahainaluna, founded by missionaries in Lahaina in 1831.

---

views of technicolored coral reefs and outlandish lava formations. A trip to the depths requires deep pockets; these 90-minute excursions aren't cheap. If the tour doesn't interest you, there is a small museum adjacent to the Atlantis office that chronicles submarine history.

And don't miss **Lahaina Jodo Mission** (661-4304), a Buddhist enclave one-half mile north of Lahaina on Ala Moana Street. There's a temple and a three-tiered pagoda here, as well as the largest ceremonial bell in Hawaii. The giant bronze Buddha, with the West Maui Mountains in the background, is a sight to behold. It rests amid stone walkways and flowering oleander bushes in a park-like setting.

For a splendid view of Lahaina, head uphill along Lahainaluna Road to **Lahainaluna School**. Established by missionaries in 1831, it is one of the country's oldest high schools. Today this historic facility serves as a public high school for the Lahaina area. On the way uphill you will pass **Pioneer Sugar Mill**, a sugar company tracing back to 1860.

LAHAINA LODGING

To fully capture the spirit of Lahaina, there's only one place to stay—the **Pioneer Inn** (658 Wharf Street; 661-3636). Located smack on Lahaina's waterfront, this rickety wooden hostelry is the center of the area's action. On one side, sloops, ketches and glass-bottom boats are berthed; on the other side lies bustling Front Street with its falsefront shops. The Inn is noisy, vibrant and crowded with tenants and tourists. On the ground floor, you can hunker down over a glass of grog at the saloon, or stroll through the Inn's lushly planted courtyard.

Upstairs are the rooms. In the older section, over the bar, dark, noisy rooms with communal and private bathrooms price in the budget range. You probably won't be able to sleep until the bar closes around 1 a.m., but you can sit on the lanai watching the moon reflect off the water. Or you can book a room in the newer, brighter and quieter section overlooking the courtyard; moderate price. Like the older digs, these are small and plainly decorated, with telephones and overhead fans. But they trade stall showers for shower-tub combinations, swap a shared lanai for a private one, provide air conditioning and add a touch of sanity to the surroundings. If you seek adventure, try the old rooms; if you value your sleep, go for the new.

While the building is actually quite modern, the **Plantation Inn** (174 Lahainaluna Road; 667-9225) possesses the look and ambience of a turn-of-the-century hostelry. Modeled after the plantation architecture of an earlier era, it features 18 rooms decorated in period. Each is adorned with poster beds, stained-glass windows and tile bathrooms. Combining the atmosphere of the past with the amenities of the present, guest rooms also feature televisions, refrigerators and air conditioning, as well as VCRs on request. There's a pool, gazebo and jacuzzi on the premises. The deluxe price tag includes a continental breakfast at the inn's restaurant.

The Oscar for most original inn goes to the **Lahaina Hotel** (127 Lahainaluna Road; 661-0577). Constructed earlier this century, this 12-room beauty was fully restored and appointed in Gay Nineties finery. Each room is wall to ceiling with gorgeous antiques—leaded glass lamps, mirrored armoires, original oil paintings, cast-iron beds and brass locks. Attention to detail is a way of life: The place simply exudes the aura of another era. If you don't stay here, stop by and visit. Deluxe.

The **Maui Islander Hotel** (660 Wainee Street; 667-9766) is a warren of woodframe buildings spread across lushly landscaped grounds. The ambience is an odd combination of tropical retreat and motel atmosphere. With 372 rooms, it's too large to be cozy. But with trimly decorated rooms and small studios (with kitchens) renting in the moderate-to-deluxe range, it's a good value. Swimming pool; laundry; tennis court; picnic area.

LAHAINA CONDOMINIUMS

Perhaps the nicest place to stay on this side of the island is **Puamana** (Pualima Place; 667-2551), a 28-acre retreat located about a mile southeast of Lahaina. This townhouse complex, a 1920s-era sugar plantation, rests along a rock-strewn beach. The oceanfront clubhouse, open to guests, was once the plantation manager's house, and the landscaped grounds are still given over to mango, plumeria and torch ginger trees. Guests stay in low-slung plantation-style buildings that sport shake-shingle roofs and house from two to six units. Prices begin in the deluxe range for one-bedroom facilities that contain kitchens and sleep up to four people. To round out the amenities there are three pools and a tennis court. Three-night minimum.

Though it's more expensive than many others, **Lahaina Shores Hotel** (475 Front Street; 661-4835) has the advantage of a beachfront location in Lahaina. This sprawling condominium complex offers studio apartments beginning at $95, while one-bedroom units start at $120. With a swimming pool and the nearby beach, it's quite convenient.

LAHAINA RESTAURANTS

One of my favorite light-food stops is a devil-may-care place called the **Sunrise Café** (located around back at 693 Front Street; 661-8558). Set in a tiny clapboard house with a fresh, airy look, it serves salads, sandwiches and espresso, but no hot entrées. Budget.

Hawaii's first phone line was installed from Lahaina to Haiku in 1877.

You'll also fare well at one of Lahaina's many shopping complexes, especially Lahaina Square on Wainee Street. Here **Amilio's Delicatessen** (661-8551) has sandwiches for vegetarians and carnivores alike. Serving practically everything that you'd expect from a self-respecting deli, the folks here do it with a special flair. Budget.

Across the street in the Lahaina Shopping Center, **Thai Chef Restaurant** (667-2814) is a cozy place with an inviting assortment of Southeast Asian dishes. Try the Korean papaya salad, duck with curry-peanut sauce, or seafood with red curry and cashews. Moderate.

Lani's Pancake Cottage (The Wharf Mall, 658 Front Street; 661-0955) has more to offer than the name implies. In addition to breakfast fare, they feature a dozen different sandwiches. Dark and cozy, with a full bar to boot, Lani's is budget-priced.

Also try **Local Food** (888 Wainee Street; 667-2882), a take-out stand that sells—what else?—local food (in the form of plate lunches). Budget.

In keeping with the old hostelry upstairs, the **Pioneer Inn Restaurant** (658 Wharf Street; 661-3636) brings back the Lahaina of old. The main dining room is a cozy anchorage dotted with nautical fixtures and specializing in regional fare. The emphasis is on the "bounty of Hawaii"; in other words, fresh fish, upcountry produce and local herbs. Select one of the day's fresh fish specials and you can't go wrong; prices are deluxe. Across the lobby, in the **Pioneer Grill and Bar**, similar but less formal fare is offered at moderate-to-deluxe prices and with a view of Lahaina Harbor. Portuguese bean soup is a specialty of both eateries and both fire their dishes on a kiawe grill.

I can't say much for the nomenclature, but the prices are worth note at **Cheeseburgers in Paradise** (811 Front Street; 661-4855). This is a rare catch indeed—an inexpensive restaurant smack on the Lahaina waterfront. Granted, you won't find much on the menu other than hamburgers, salads and sandwiches. But if some couples can live on love, why can't the rest of us live on ocean views? Budget to moderate.

For a taste of the Orient, I'd head to the Lahaina Shopping Center (Wainee Street between Papalua Street and Lahainaluna Road) and the **Golden Palace Chinese Restaurant** (661-3126). Boldly decorated with Chinese reliefs, this dimly lit establishment has an extensive Cantonese menu. There are beef, fowl, pork and seafood dishes, as well as chop suey. In the afternoon, the Palace combines sweet-and-sour ribs, roast pork, chop suey, shrimp and rice. Moderate.

Nearby, in the same complex, is **Musashi Japanese Cuisine** (Lahaina Shopping Center; 667-6207). Highly regarded by area residents, it has a sushi bar and table seating. Prices are moderate to deluxe, and the menu includes a full selection of standard Japanese dishes. Lunch and dinner on weekdays; dinner only on the weekends.

Dine on the upper level at the **Tree House Restaurant** (Lahaina Market Place, Front Street and Lahainaluna Road; 661-3235) and you'll catch a breeze through the branches. This Swiss Family Robinson-style dining place specializes in shrimp and chicken dishes with a few fresh fish entrées added for good measure. Moderate prices make it a good value.

Offering a partial view of the water at moderate prices is **Moondoggies** (666 Front Street; 661-3966). This balcony restaurant is on the wrong side of Front Street but does provide an easy, you-can-sit-at-the-bar-or-take-a-table atmosphere. Wherever you rest your okole, you can dine on pupus, pasta, pizza, sandwiches, soups or salad.

If you've seen one **Hard Rock Café** (900 Front Street; 667-7400) you know about the line for the T-shirt window, the line for a table and the line for the bar. What a formula: Just get yourself a show car from the '50s, a few surfboards, guitars and Buddy Holly posters, throw in an exposed-beam ceiling and circular bar and you've got the Maui branch of this popular empire. The menu runs from beef, turkey and veggie burgers to lime barbecue chicken, marinated top sirloin and fajitas. Moderate.

Light, bright and airy, **Compadres** (Front and Kapunakea streets, in the Lahaina Cannery Mall; 661-7189) is a great place to sip a margarita or enjoy a Mexican meal with an island flair. The tropical ambience is as appealing as the steaming dishes served here. Especially popular are the fajitas and pork carnitas, but the menu also offers burgers, salads and vegetarian dishes. Moderate.

The preferred style of dining in Lahaina is steak and seafood at one of the waterfront restaurants along Front Street. And the common denominator is the ever-popular, usually crowded **Kimo's** (845 Front Street; 661-4811), where you can enjoy all the tropical amenities while dining on seafood fettucine, lobster or prime rib. Moderate.

Personally, I prefer the **Lahaina Broiler** (889 Front Street; 661-3111), a more stylish address where you can experience the same open-air atmosphere. Offering a fresh fish special, as well as an assortment of beef and chicken entrées, it prices in the moderate-to-deluxe category.

Slightly (I said *slightly*) off the tourist track but still offering a classic Lahaina-dinner-on-the-water-with-sunset-view experience is the **Old Lahaina Café and Luau** (505 Front Street; 661-3303). Overhead fans, oceanfront location, nautical feel—it's all here. The menu matches the occasion with fresh island fish, jumbo prawns (prepared five different ways) and a special Hawaiian sampler. Also open for breakfast and lunch; moderate to deluxe.

Upstairs in a modest building, **Alex's Hole in the Wall** (835 Front Street, down Wahie Lane; 661-3197) is where knowledgeable diners sacrifice grand views for the pleasures of family-style Italian cooking. Fresh pasta, homemade sausage and traditional family recipes have kept this spot in business for years. Deluxe-priced entrées include manicotti and meatballs, veal piccata, shrimp alfredo, pasta primavera, and linguine and sausage. You'll also find innovative specials and children's portions.

At **Longhi's** (888 Front Street; 667-2288), a European-style café that also specializes in Italian dishes, informality is the password. The menu changes daily and is never written down; the waiter simply tells you the day's offerings. Usually there'll be several pasta dishes, sautéed vegetables, salads, a shellfish creation, steak, a wine-soaked chicken or veal dish and perhaps eggplant parmigiana. Longhi's prepares all of its own bread and pasta, buys Maui-grown produce and imports many cheeses from New York. The dinners, reflect this diligence. Breakfasts and lunches are cooked with the same care. Definitely recommended, especially for vegetarians, who can choose from many of the dishes offered. Deluxe to ultra-deluxe.

Hawaiian regional cuisine is the order of the day at **Avalon Restaurant & Bar** (844 Front Street; 667-5559), an open-air establishment in Mariner's Alley. Adorned with the work of local artists, it is owned by Mark and Judy Ellman. Mark is the master chef—preparing wok-fried *opakapaka* in black bean sauce, Chinese duck with plum sauce and other delectables—while Judy greets the folks out front. Try it for lunch or dinner; deluxe.

David Paul's Lahaina Grill (127 Lahainaluna Road; 667-5117), headlining New American cuisine (with a Southwestern accent), is an intimate dining room with a personalized touch. According to owner/chef David Paul, the menu represents "a gathering of technique, flavors and skills from around the world, utilizing local ingredients to translate each dish into an exceptional dining experience." Order the tequila shrimp and fire cracker rice, soft-shell crabs, Kona coffee-roasted rack of lamb or macadamia-smoked tenderloin and decide for yourself whether he carries it off. Deluxe to ultra-deluxe.

The defining experience in Lahaina dining is **Gerard's Restaurant** (174 Lahainaluna Road; 661-8939). Here you'll encounter a French restaurant in a colonial setting with tropical surroundings. Housed in the Plantation Inn, a bed and breakfast reminiscent of early New Orleans, Gerard's provides a chandelier-and-pattern-wallpaper dining room as well as a veranda complete with overhead fans and whitewashed balustrade. The chef prepares fresh fish, rack of lamb, calf veal liver, *confit* of duck and puff pastry with shiitake mushrooms. Of course, that is after having started off with ahi steak tartar or crab bisque. Ultra-deluxe.

Overlooking the Mala Wharf, **The Chart House** (1450 Front Street; 661-0937) looks as indigenous as a Hawaiian sunset. With its shake roof, lava walls and *koa* decor, this veranda-style restaurant is perfect for a drink or dinner. Dine on sirloin, teriyaki beef kabobs, shrimp scampi or

Hawaiian chicken. There's also a handy children's menu. Offering views of Lanai and Molokai, the restaurant is a perfect retreat after a hard day of surfing or sunning. Deluxe.

Near the top of the cognoscenti's list of gourmet establishments is an unlikely looking French restaurant in Olowalu called **Chez Paul** (Honoapiilani Highway; 661-3843). The place is several miles outside Lahaina in a dilapidated building that also houses Olowalu's funky general store. But for years this little hideaway has had a reputation far transcending its surroundings. You'll probably drive right past the place at first, but when you do find it, you'll discover a menu featuring such delicacies as *tournedos*, duck *à l'orange*, veal prepared with apples, scampi and several other tempting entrées. While the tab runs in the ethereal ultra-deluxe range, the rave reviews this prim dining room receives make it worth every franc.

LAHAINA SHOPPING

Lahaina's a great place to combine shopping with sightseeing. Most shops are right on Front Street in the historic wooden buildings facing the water. For a walking tour of the stores and waterfront, start from the Pioneer Inn at the south end of the strip and walk north on the makai or ocean side. Then come back along the mauka or mountain side of the street.

One of the first shops you will encounter on this consumer's tour of Lahaina will be **Sgt. Leisure Resort Patrol** (701 Front Street; 667-0661), which has an array of imaginative T-shirts.

The Gecko Store (703 Front Street; 661-1078), the only shop I've seen with a sand floor, also stocks inexpensive beachwear, as well as T-shirts and toys. The **Endangered Species Store** (707 Front Street; 661-0208), which features a multitude of conservation-minded items such as oils and lotions from the rainforest, is a worthy stop. You will also find *koa*-framed posters, chimes, statues and a healthy supply of T-shirts and stuffed animals.

Past the sea wall, in an overgrown cottage set back from the street, lie several shops including **Pacific Vision** (819 Front Street; 661-0188), with its hand-etched glass and crystal pieces. And just down the street at **South Seas Trading Post** (780 Front Street; 661-3168), you can barter greenbacks for Nepali wedding necklaces, Chinese porcelain opium pillows or New Guinea masks.

There are just a few more street numbers before this shopper's promenade ends. Then if you cross the road and walk back in the opposite direction, with the sea to your right, you'll pass **The Gallery** (716 Front Street; 661-0696), which has jade and pearl pieces among its inventory of exotic jewelry. You'll also find antiques and artworks at this unusual shop.

Nearby at **The Wharf** (658 Front Street) mall, there's a maze of stores. Try **The Whaler's Book Shoppe** (667-9544) for an unbeatable

In the mid-1800s, Lahaina was the whaling capital of the world. Today one might call it the whale-watching capital.

combination—good books and fine coffee. One of the best bookstores around, it doubles as a coffeehouse where you can sit back, read and sip a cup of Kona brew. One shop at The Wharf worth a look is **Seegerpeople** (658 Front Street; 661-1084). Essentially a portrait studio, this store adds a twist to an otherwise traditional craft. Instead of being framed, the pictures are mounted on quarter-inch-thick Lucite, cut out in the shape of the subject and placed on a base. The result is a freestanding "photosculpture" and humorous keepsake.

Village Gallery has two stores in Lahaina (120 Dickenson Street, 661-4402; Lahaina Cannery, Front and Kapunakea streets, 661-3280), both featuring paintings by modern Hawaiian artists. Amid the tourist schlock there is some brilliant artwork.

Also stop in at the **Lahaina Art Society** (649 Wharf Street, beneath the Old Courthouse; 661-0111). This is a great place if you're in the market for local artwork; on display are pieces by a number of Maui artists.

The **Lahaina Cannery Mall** (1221 Honoapiilani Highway; 661-5304), a massive complex of stores housed in an old canning factory, is the area's most ambitious project. **Lahaina Printsellers** (667-7843), one of my favorite Maui shops, has an astounding collection of ancient maps and engravings from Polynesia and other parts of the world. **Alexia Natural Fashions** (661-4110) offers stylish women's clothing from the island of Cyprus and other romantic locales.

Another major shopping mall, **Lahaina Center** (corner of Front and Papalana streets) is a sprawling complex of theaters, shops and restaurants. **Kite Fantasy** (661-4766) is the place to pick up stunt and sport kites including diamond, box and bird designs. Here you'll also find wind socks, mobiles, boomerangs, kaleidoscopes, games and a wide array of windup toys. Complete flying instructions, including tips on where to launch your kite, are provided by the helpful staff. **Mama and Me** (661-6165) specializes in traditional Hawaiiana. Original photos of Maui's finest hula dancers, together with antiques, shell necklaces and a wide variety of art objects are sold. Among the simple treasures are *koa* sculptures, baskets, tapa cloth and other fine craft pieces.

Dickenson Square (Dickenson and Wainee streets) represents another theme mall, fashioned after an early 20th-century plantation manor.

Built to resemble a New England fishing village, **505 Front Street**, located at 505 Front Street, is an attractive woodframe mall. Situated south of central Lahaina, it is home to almost two dozen shops, including galleries, boutiques and jewelry stores.

LAHAINA NIGHTLIFE

Front Street's the strip in Lahaina—a dilapidated row of buildings from which stream some of the freshest sounds around.

Moondoggies (666 Front Street; 661-3966) has live music playing seven days a week. There's an evening show to accompany dinner as well as a late show. Different musicians, playing sounds that range from country Hawaiian to contemporary rock-and-roll, are always featured.

The place of places along this surging waterfront is **Longhi's** (888 Front Street; 667-2288). The upper story of this well-known restaurant is painted brilliant white and decorated in a startling black-and-white motif; the dancefloor is native *koa* wood. The result is a club that draws a jet-set crowd. You'll hear a local jazz or rock group working out on stage every Friday and Saturday from 10:30 p.m. to 1:30 a.m. Cover.

Over at the **Pioneer Bar and Grill** (661-3636), the standard fare is blues and jazz. Tucked into a corner of the Pioneer Inn, this spot features a sea going motif complete with harpoons, figureheads and other historical nautical decor. Usually packed to the bulkheads with a lively crew, it's a great place to hunker down over a glass of rum.

Moose McGillycuddy's (844 Front Street; 667-7758) is a hot club offering a large dancefloor and a variety of live music acts. The house is congenial and the drinks imaginatively mixed; for contemporary sounds with dinner, arrive before 10 p.m. Cover.

Lahaina's favorite pastime is watching the sun set over the ocean while sipping a tall, cool one at a waterfront watering place. Prime places for this very rewarding activity are **Kimo's** (845 Front Street; 661-4811), which also features a range of live music, and the **Lahaina Broiler** (885 Front Street; 661-3111). After the sun finishes performing, the Lahaina Broiler features do-it-yourself karaoke entertainment.

A musical showcase that starts the evening with big band tunes and then accelerates through the decades to the 1990s, **Blue Tropix** (900 Front Street; 667-5309) is one of Maui's most popular nightclubs. This high-tech Los Angeles-style club is done in basic black and chrome and features a circular bar and planetarium ceiling. If that's not enough, you'll also find a huge dancefloor, 11 video screens and a gourmet kitchen. Most of the music emanates from a deejay, but live rock bands appear on Tuesday nights. Come check out the in crowd. There's a cover charge after 9 p.m.

If it's Friday, you can also browse the art galleries of Lahaina, which sponsor a special **Art Night** every week.

For an awe-inspiring glimpse into Hawaii's past, watch the 40-minute film at the **Omni Theatre/Hawaii Experience** (824 Front Street; 661-8314). Offering a three-dimensional perspective of the state's history, this film is shown on a huge domed 180-degree screen.

LAHAINA BEACHES AND PARKS

Kiawe trees and scrub vegetation spread right to the shoreline along **Papalaua Wayside Park**. There are sandy patches between the trees large enough to spread a towel, but I prefer sunbathing at beaches closer to Lahaina. This narrow beach, which is about ten miles south of Lahaina, is bounded on one side by Honoapiilani Highway and extends for a mile to join a nicer, lawn-fringed park; then it stretches on toward Olowalu for several more miles. If you want to be alone, just head down the shore. Swimming is good, snorkeling is okay out past the surf break and surfing is excellent at Thousand Peaks breaks and also very good several miles east in Maalaea Bay. There's an outhouse and picnic area at the state wayside and picnic facilities at the grassy park.

The **Olowalu Beaches** are narrow corridors of white sand north and south of Olowalu General Store. To get there, go south from Lahaina on Honoapiilani Highway for about six miles. This is an excellent area to hunt for Maui diamonds. Swimming is very good and south of the general store, where road and water meet, you'll find an excellent coral reef for snorkeling. Surfers will find good breaks with right and left slides about a half-mile north of the general store. Ulua are often caught from Olowalu landing. There are no facilities, but there is a market nearby.

A seaside lawn shaded by palm trees, **Launiupoko Wayside Park** has no beach. The park, three miles south of Lahaina on Honoapiilani Highway, is near the West Maui Mountains, with great views of Kahoolawe and Lanai. A rock seawall slopes gently for entering swimmers, but offers little to sunbathers. Swimming and snorkeling are mediocre. There is good surf-casting from the seawall and south for three miles. The park has a picnic area, restrooms and showers.

A grass-covered strip with ironwood trees and a narrow beach wedged between Honoapiilani Highway and the ocean, **Puamana State Wayside Park** (Honoapiilani Highway, two miles south of Lahaina) offers excellent views that make this a choice spot for an enjoyable picnic.

The one thing going for **Maluulu O Lele Park** is its convenient location in Lahaina, right on Front Street next to the 505 Front Street mall. Otherwise, it's heavily littered, shadowed by the mall and sometimes crowded. If you do stop by, try to forget all that and concentrate on the sandy beach, lawn and truly startling view of Lanai directly across the Auau Channel. Swimming is okay, snorkeling good past the reef and, for surfing, there are breaks in the summer near the seawall in Lahaina Harbor. This surfing spot is not for beginners! Threadfin and *ulua* are common catches here. Restrooms and tennis courts are across the street near the playing field.

The best beach in Lahaina is a curving stretch of white sand called **Baby Beach**. It lacks privacy but certainly not beauty. From here you can look back to Lahaina town and the West Maui Mountains or out over the ocean to Kahoolawe, Lanai and Molokai. Or just close your eyes and soak up the sun. Take Front Street north from Lahaina for about a half-mile. Turn left on Puunoa Place and follow it to the beach. Swimming is good and well protected, if shallow. Snorkeling is only fair. In summer there are breaks nearby at Mala Wharf; left slide. Threadfin and ulua are often caught. There are restrooms and showers at the beach.

There are facilities aplenty in **Wahikuli Wayside Park**, which might be why this pretty spot is so popular and crowded. A narrow stretch of beach and lawn, just off the road between Lahaina and Kaanapali, it faces Lanai and Molokai. Swimming is very good, but snorkeling only fair. (There's a better spot just north of here near the Lahaina Canoe Club.) The most common catches here are *ulua* and threadfin. Facilities include picnic areas and restrooms; there are tennis courts up the street at the Civic Center.

Conveniently located beside Kaanapali Beach Resort on Honoapii-lani Highway between Lahaina and Kaanapali, **Hanakaoo Beach Park** is long and narrow, with a white-sand beach and grassy picnic ground. The road is nearby, but the views of Lanai are outstanding. Swimming is good, snorkeling fair, but surfing poor. Common catches include *ulua* and threadfin. There are picnic areas, restrooms and showers.

SHELL HUNTING

With over 1500 varieties of shells washing up on its beaches, Hawaii has some of the world's finest shelling. The miles of sandy beach along Maui's south shore are a prime area for handpicking free souvenirs. Along the shores are countless shell specimens with names like horned helmet, Hebrew cone, Hawaiian olive and Episcopal miter. Or you might find glass balls from Japan and sunbleached driftwood.

Beachcombing is the easiest method of shell gathering. Take along a small container and stroll through the backwash of the waves, watching for ripples from shells lying under the sand. You can also dive in shallow water where the ocean's surge will uncover shells.

It's tempting to walk along the top of coral reefs seeking shells and other marine souvenirs, but these living formations maintain a delicate ecological balance. Reefs in Hawaii and all over the planet are dying because of such plunder. In order to protect this underwater world, try to collect only shells and souvenirs that are adrift on the beach and no longer necessary to the marine ecology.

The best shelling spots along Maui's south shore are Makena, Kihei beaches, Maalaea Bay, Olowalu, the sandy stretch from Kaanapali to Napili Bay, D. T. Fleming Park and Honolua Bay. On the north coast, the stretch from Waiehu to Waihee (west of Kahului) and the beaches around Hana are the choicest hunting grounds.

After heavy rainfall, watch near stream mouths for Hawaiian olivines and in stream beds for Maui diamonds. Olivines are small, semiprecious stones of an olive hue. Maui diamonds are quartz stones and make beautiful jewelry. The best places to go diamond hunting are near the Kahului Bay hotel strip and in Olowalu Stream.

FIVE

Kaanapali-Kapalua Area

Even in the case of Maui's notorious land developers, there is method to
the madness. The stretch of coastline extending for six miles along
Maui's western shore, crowded to the extreme with hotels and condominiums, is anchored by two planned resorts. Like handsome bookends
supporting an uneven array of dog-eared paperbacks, Kaanapali and Kapalua add class to the arrangement.

Supporting the south end, **Kaanapali** is a 500-acre enclave that extends along three miles of sandy beach and includes six hotels, a half-
dozen condominiums, two golf courses and an attractive shopping mall.
Back in the 19th century it was a dry and barren segment of the sugar
plantation that operated from Lahaina. Raw sugar was hauled by train
from the mill out to Black Rock, a dramatic outcropping along Kaanapali Beach, where the produce was loaded onto waiting ships.

In 1962, Kaanapali's first resort opened near Black Rock and development soon spread in both directions. Important to developers,
who built the Sheraton Maui hotel around it, **Black Rock** (Puu Kekaa)
is a volcanic cinder cone from which ancient Hawaiians believed that
the dead departed the earth in their journey to the spirit world. According to legend, the great 18th-century Maui chief Kahekili proved his
bravery by leaping from the rock to the ocean below.

Kaanapali's modern-day contribution to Pacific culture is the **Whalers Village Museum** (Whalers Village, 2435 Kaanapali Parkway; 661-
5992). A three-part facility comprised of an outdoor pavilion and two
buildings connected by a sky-bridge, the museum details Lahaina's history of whaling and explains the physiology of Hawaii's beloved humpback. Outdoors, you'll find a 30-foot long whale skeleton and a whaling

---

On an average day, 38,000 tourists enjoy the good life on Maui.

---

longboat on display. The "golden era of whaling" is also portrayed in scrimshaw exhibits, a scale model whaling ship, harpoons and other artifacts from the days when Lahaina was one of the world's great whaling ports.

An earlier chief, Piilani, built a road through the area in the 16th century and gave his name to modern-day Route 30, the Honoapiilani Highway. Translated as "the bays of Piilani," the road passes several inlets located north of Kaanapali that have been developed in haphazard fashion. Honokowai, Kahana and Napili form a continuous wall of condominiums that sprawls north to Kapalua Bay and offer West Maui's best lodging bargains.

Kapalua, the bookend holding the north side in place, is a former pineapple plantation that was converted into a luxurious 1500-acre resort. Here two major hotels, three golf courses and several villa-style communities blanket the hillside from the white sands of Kapalua Bay to the deep-green foothills of the West Maui Mountains. Like the entire strip along Maui's western flank, Kapalua enjoys otherworldly sunsets and dramatic views of Lanai and Molokai.

KAANAPALI-KAPALUA AREA LODGING

In the Kaanapali area the modestly priced hotel is not an endangered species, it's totally extinct! The closest you will come to a money-saving facility is the **Kaanapali Beach Hotel** (2525 Kaanapali Parkway; 661-0011). This 430-room hostelry sits right on the beach, sports many restaurants and a large lobby, and rents rooms in the deluxe-to-ultra-deluxe range. Guest rooms enjoy private lanais and guests lounge around a grassy courtyard and a swimming pool.

Or check out, and check in to, the **Royal Lahaina Resort** (2780 Kekaa Drive, Kaanapali; 661-3611). Spreading across 27 acres, it encompasses 542 rooms, 11 tennis courts, three swimming pools, two restaurants and a white-sand beach that extends for a half-mile. Rooms in the highrise hotel price in the ultra-deluxe category, while the prices for the nicest accommodations, the multiplex cottages that dot the landscaped grounds, head for the sky.

In the realm of luxury hotels, the **Hyatt Regency Maui** (200 Nohea Kai Drive, Kaanapali; 661-1234) is one of the better addresses in Hawaii. Built in 1980, its atrium lobby, Asian artwork and freeform swimming pool have set the standard for deluxe resorts ever since. Unlike more recent hotels, in which the size of guest rooms is sacrificed for the sake of

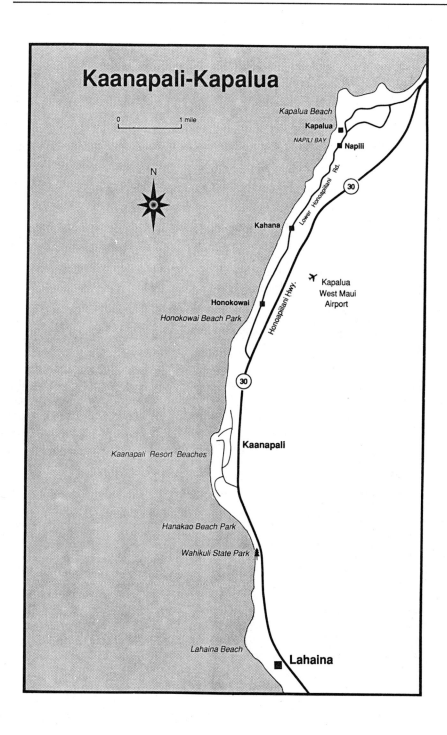

Kaanapali-Kapalua

0 _____ 1 mile

N

Kapalua Beach

■ **Kapalua**

NAPILI BAY   ■ **Napili**

30

Lower Honoapiilani Rd.

Kahana ■

✈ Kapalua
West Maui
Airport

Honokowai ■

Honoapiilani Hwy.

Honokowai Beach Park

30

Kaanapali Resort Beaches

Kaanapali

Hanakao Beach Park

Wahikuli State Park

Lahaina Beach   ■ **Lahaina**

lavish grounds, the Hyatt Regency maintains an ideal balance between public and private areas. If you're seeking beautiful surroundings, friendly service and beachfront location at ultra-deluxe prices, this 812-room extravaganza is the ticket.

There's no check-in line at the **Maui Marriott** (100 Nohea Kai Drive, Kaanapali; 667-8226). Thanks to an advance registration system, guests simply pick up their keys and head to one of 720 rooms or suites in the nine-story Lanai or Molokai wings. This atrium-style hotel comes with all the amenities you'd expect at an ultra-deluxe-priced Kaanapali resort including two swimming pools, five tennis courts, an arcade of shops, beautiful gardens and a beachfront setting. Pastels and earth tones highlight spacious rooms adorned with rattan and bleached-pine furniture, lanais and marble baths. Despite the amenities, the Marriott does not match the illustrious competition that lies along Kaanapali Beach.

With $2 million worth of art gracing the public areas, five free-form pools, 20-foot waterfalls and pink Chilean flamingos in the gardens, the ultra-deluxe-priced **Westin Maui** (2365 Kaanapali Parkway, Kaanapali; 667-2525) is the kind of place that comes with its own director of romance. Hawaiian sculptures and marble baths grace the rooms and from the lanais you'll enjoy postcard views of the mountains or ocean. One of Maui's most elegant hotels, the 761-room Westin Maui offers six restaurants and lounges and even provides tours of its art collection and resident wildlife.

At Black Rock, the sacred lava promontory where cliff divers plunged into the Pacific, the ancient tradition is re-enacted as part of a nightly torch-lighting ceremony at the **Sheraton Maui Kaanapali Beach Resort** (2605 Kaanapali Parkway, Kaanapali; 661-0031). Here 495 rooms and suites are spread across spacious grounds that hold two six-story towers, an Ocean Lanai wing and a colony of cottages. The hotel's distinctive architecture—it is partially built atop the rock—places some rooms near the water's edge. Views of the neighbor islands and the West Maui Mountains are breathtaking. Decorated with rattan furni-

---

ABOVE MAUI

*High atop the Hyatt Regency Maui's Lahaina Tower, a 16-inch reflecting telescope probes deep space five nights a week, taking tourists on a trip through the planets and galaxies. The **Tour of the Stars** (200 Nohea Kai Drive, Kaanapali; 661-1234; admission), a one-hour program managed by the hotel's director of astronomy and designed for the public, allows guests to look through stationary eyepieces while the computer-driven telescope searches the heavens. Reservations are required.*

Not more than ten miles from the elegant Kapalua area are places so rugged they have rarely been explored.

ture, tropical prints and seashell-patterned bedspreads, all the rooms are trim and comfortable. You can watch the sunset from several restaurants and lounges, swim in your choice of pools or enjoy snorkeling along Black Rock. Ultra-deluxe. (The Sheraton Maui is closed for renovation from January 1995 until November 1996.)

A waterfall plunges down the side of one of the three atrium towers at **Embassy Suites Resort** (104 Kaanapali Shores Place, Kaanapali; 661-2000). Not impressed? How about enough macaws, golden mantled rosellas and sulphur-crested cockatoos to make you think you have checked into an aviary rather than an all-suite hotel. Hop aboard a glass-walled elevator and luxuriate in one of the 413 units. Each one is spacious, attractive and equipped with candy-striped sofas, oak cabinets and Casablanca fans. You'll have a lanai and large bath of your own and to share with other guests there is a 24-foot waterslide and gazebo pavilion, carp ponds and waterways galore. Besides that, breakfast is free and you're invited to a daily cocktail reception. Ultra-deluxe.

A subtle architectural style gives the **Kapalua Bay Hotel** (1 Bay Drive, Kapalua; 669-5656) a low profile. But don't be misled. Part of a 23,000-acre plantation, this relatively small hotel, with 194 rooms and suites, is the hub of one of Maui's most appealing resorts. A hillside setting overlooking a white-sand crescent beach means that nearly all the rooms have spectacular ocean views. The accommodations are luxurious and tasteful and include rattan- and wicker-furnished sitting areas, marble baths with sunken tubs, and vanity areas. Floor-to-ceiling french doors open onto spacious lanais. Rock-lined ponds, tropical gardens, three golf courses, restaurants, shops and a tennis facility add to Kapalua's charm. This ultra-deluxe-priced resort is one of Maui's most romantic.

Spread across 37 acres in the historic Honokahua region, the **Ritz-Carlton Kapalua** (1 Ritz-Carlton Drive, Kapalua; 669-6200) has incorporated plantation-style architecture into its elegant resort. This 550-room ultra-deluxe-priced property is part of the Kapalua resort complex. The posh wood-paneled lobby is illuminated with chandeliers and hurricane lamps. Overstuffed plaid print furniture, marble desks, porcelain lamps and double vanities highlight the rooms and suites. All have ocean views from their lanais. You can explore trails of the ancients and visit old wooden churches. To help preserve Maui's heritage, the hotel has set aside a 14-acre sanctuary where Hawaiians perform cultural and religious ceremonies. Situated above a sandy beach, the Ritz-Carlton also offers a well-landscaped, three-level pool.

KAANAPALI-KAPALUA AREA CONDOMINIUMS

Most condominiums in this area are on the beach or just across the road from it. They are ideally situated for swimming or sunbathing; the major drawback, ironically, is that there are so many other condos around.

Kaanapali Alii (50 Nohea Kai Drive, Kaanapali; 667-1400) ranks as one of Maui's better buys. Here the immense 1500- to 1900-square-foot suites can easily be shared by two couples or a family. All 210 condo units have large living and dining rooms, full kitchens, sitting areas and two baths. Fully carpeted and furnished with rattan, contemporary artwork and potted palms, these units start as low as $145 (including a car) and top out at $450. Room service comes from the adjacent Maui Marriott. The contemporary high-rise facility rests along the beach and has a pool and tennis court.

Adjacent to the shops of Whaler's Village, **The Whaler on Kaanapali Beach** (2481 Kaanapali Parkway, Kaanapali; 661-4861) offers spacious units with *koa* parquet floors and rattan furniture. With its twin 12-story towers, this oceanfront condominium boasts marble baths and has 170 units priced from $160 to $345.

For its 204 condominium units, **Maui Eldorado Resort** (2661 Kekaa Drive, Kaanapali; 661-0021) has a golf-course setting a short distance from the beach. The rooms, ranging from $116 to $240 per day, are decorated with a tropical motif, furnished in wicker and equipped with large baths, lanais and vanities. Low-rise buildings in the complex offer a peaceful alternative to the busy hotel scene. Residents enjoy three swimming pools and a private beach club on the sands of Kaanapali.

KIDS IN KAANAPALI

*It's camp time in Kaanapali. The advantage of staying at one of the major resorts in the area is freedom! Freedom for your kids to get away from you while you are enjoying a short respite from the little darlings, knowing that they are being entertained. At the **Hyatt Regency Maui,** kids from three to 12 can join Camp Hyatt where their day will be filled with arts and crafts, scavenger hunts and an introduction to Hawaiian culture. Rock Hyatt for teenagers includes horseback riding, sailing, shopping and teen nightclubs. The Keiki Camp at **Maui Marriott** includes lei making, hula classes and field trips to Lahaina. A special creative movement and pre-ballet class for young children is offered at the **Westin Maui**, which also offers a wildlife program, snorkeling classes and teen sailing excursions. At the **Embassy Suites Resort,** kids learn local legends, explore tidepools and build a Hawaiian-style kite. Ritz-Kids at the **Ritz-Carlton Kapalua** offers aerobic exercise, croquet tournaments, basket weaving and a special dinner theater. Too bad we're not all kids.*

Far from being all condos and malls, Maui is home to 600 farms.

The lava rock-walled units at **Papakea Beach Resort** (3543 Lower Honoapiilani Road, Honokowai; 669-4848) provide a pleasant retreat. Ranging from $130 studios to $204 two-bedroom units, all 120 condos come with spacious lanais. Though individually decorated, all the units are appointed with tropical prints, pastel-colored lamps and oak and rattan furniture. Although there is no swimming beach on the property, this resort has an attractive pool area, spa, tennis court and putting green.

The **Napili Kai Beach Club** (5900 Honoapiilani Road, Napili Bay; 669-6271) has 162 units—studios, one-bedroom and two-bedroom affairs—that range in price from $155 to $450. Most come with kitchens. All are fully carpeted and have private lanais, rattan furniture, picture windows and direct access to an impressive beach. This resort is perfectly situated for golf, tennis and snorkeling.

Aston Kaanapali Shores (3445 Lower Honoapiilani Road, Honokowai; 667-2211) has hotel-room-style accommodations for $119 including refrigerator, microwave and a wet bar; studios from $159 double ($129 from April 1 to December 21) with a balcony and full kitchen; and one-bedroom units with a garden view and full kitchen for $189. They may be large and expensive, but these units are right at the entrance to Honokowai Beach and have two pools, jacuzzis, tennis courts, fitness center, restaurant and shops. They also have a year-round activities program for children three and up.

Providing an excellent deal, **Kapalua Villas** (500 Office Road, Kapalua; 669-8088) are situated on a golf course and offer prices that start at just $145 ($175 in the peak winter season). The setting is tranquil and the views sweep past the mountains, Oneloa Bay and neighbor islands. The units are low-rise structures with sunken tubs, large lanais and rattan and wicker furniture. Individually decorated, the accommodations provide direct access to swimming, golf and tennis. Oceanview and oceanfront villas range from $195 to $275; two-bedroom units run from $195 to $375.

The following are additional facilities. They are more economical, but I think you'll find that they meet basic requirements for comfort and convenience.

Maui Sands (3600 Lower Honoapiilani Road, Kaanapali; 669-1902). One-bedroom apartments begin at $80 single or double; two bedrooms run $100 for one to four people. There is a seven-night minimum. Beachfront.

Paki Maui (3615 Lower Honoapiilani Road, Kaanapali; 669-8235). One-bedroom apartments run from $139 to $159, depending on the view, and sleep one to four people; two-bedroom units start at $199, accommodating up to six people. Jacuzzi. Oceanfront.

Aston Maui Park (3626 Lower Honoapiilani Road, Honokowai; 669-6622). Studios from $89 ($79 from April 1 to December 21). Across the street from the beach.

Honokowai Palms (3666 Lower Honoapiilani Road, Honokowai; 669-6130). One-bedroom apartments (up to four people) with lanai and ocean view run $65 double. Two-bedroom units without lanai are $75 for one to six people. Located right across the street from the ocean.

Hale Maui (3711 Lower Honoapiilani Road, Honokowai; 669-6312) has one-bedroom condos for $65 double. On the waterfront; no pool.

Kaleialoha (3785 Lower Honoapiilani Road, Honokowai; 669-8197). One-bedroom apartments are $85 double; $7.50 each additional person. Oceanfront.

Hale Ono Loa (3823 Lower Honoapiilani Road, Honokowai; 669-9680) offers one-bedroom units at $85 for up to four people and two-bedroom units for $150. Oceanfront but no beach.

Polynesian Shores (3975 Lower Honoapiilani Road, Honokowai; 669-6065). One-bedroom apartments start at $95 double; two-bedroom units, $119 double; three-bedroom apartments, $159 double. All units have ocean view.

Mahina Surf (4057 Lower Honoapiilani Road, Kahana; 669-6068). One-bedroom units start at $110 double ($85 from April 15 to December 14); two-bedroom accommodations are $130 and $105, respectively. Oceanfront on a lava-rock beach.

Kahana Reef (4471 Lower Honoapiilani Road, Kahana; 669-6491). Studio apartments, $85 single or double; one-bedroom apartments are $90 single or double; $15 more from December 19 to Easter. All units are oceanfront and have daily maid service.

Napili Point Resort (5295 Lower Honoapiilani Road, Napili; 669-9222). One-bedroom condos are $164 for up to four people ($134 from

---

IN THE BEGINNING

*Today, resort hotels on Maui cost more than $500,000 per room to build. Talk about inflation. The island's first large resort, the 210-room **Sheraton Maui**, was constructed for $4.75 million or about $22,600 a room in 1963. Amfac, the developer, expected other hotel giants to rush in immediately and build similar resorts after the Sheraton opened. When they didn't, the company put up $10 million to build the area's second major property, **Kaanapali Beach Resort**. That created the critical mass necessary to attract a flurry of developers, all building at a fraction of today's prices.*

April 20 to December 21). Here sliding doors lead out to ocean-view patios. Located on a lava rock beach, the resort is a short walk from sandy Napili Bay beach.

Colony's Napili Shores (5315 Honoapiilani Road, Napili; 669-8061) is a beautifully landscaped low-rise resort with studios and one-bedrooms running from $135 to $185. The units are appointed with rattan and oak pieces and the complex is graced by gardens of plumeria and hibiscus. The pool and beach areas are idyllic.

The Napili Bay (33 Hui Drive, Napili; 669-6044). Studio apartments are $95 double for garden and partial ocean views and $125 for oceanfront. Rates drop to the $75-$100 range in the off-season.

KAANAPALI-KAPALUA AREA RESTAURANTS

Luigi's Pasta & Pizzeria (661-3160) is located near the entrance to Kaanapali Beach Resort. A patio restaurant overlooking a golf course, it's a pretty place to dine on pizza, pasta and other Italian favorites. Open for dinner only, the restaurant features a menu that includes veal marsala, chicken parmesan and shrimp scampi. Moderate.

The **Kaanapali Beach Hotel Koffee Shop** (Kaanapali Beach Hotel; 661-0011) serves an all-you-can-eat buffet at a price that is surprisingly out of place for this expensive hotel. But don't expect too much for so little. The menu is limited to a few egg dishes at breakfast, sandwiches and a few entrées for lunch and dinner. Budget to moderate.

Spats II (Hyatt Regency Maui, Kaanapali Beach Resort; 661-1234) is an elegant Italian restaurant featuring regional cuisine. Marble table-tops, antique armchairs and brass chandeliers are just some of the decorations, which are augmented by a deluxe-to-ultra-deluxe-priced menu of decadent dishes such as lobster on ribbon pasta covered with an herb cream sauce.

Overlooking serene Japanese gardens, the open-air **Swan Court** (200 Nohea Kai Drive, Kaanapali Beach; 661-1234) defines the ultimate Maui experience. Guests enter this upscale restaurant in the Hyatt Regency Maui via a grand staircase to the classical strains of the resident pianist. With a waterfall and gliding swans in the background, you can choose from a variety of entrées such as smoked salmon and ahi, bisque of Kauai prawns in cream and cognac, fresh island fish baked on a plate of oak-wood, or roasted crisp duckling with maple tamarind glaze. For dessert, try the seasonal fruits and berries between crisp filo layers. Ultra-deluxe.

Chico's Cantina (Whalers Village; 667-2777) is one of those tacky theme restaurants that prove either entertaining or annoying, depending on your disposition and mood. Surfboards tacked to the wall, a car in the middle of the restaurant—that sort of thing. If you manage to get as far as the food, you'll find fajitas, chimichangas, burritos and other budget-to-moderate-priced Mexican dishes.

You can dine by the water at **Leilani's On The Beach** (Whalers Village; 661-4495). The sunsets are otherworldly at this breezy veranda-style dining room. Trimmed in dark woods and lava rock, it's dominated by an outrigger canoe that hangs suspended from the ceiling. On the menu you'll find Malaysian shrimp, spinach and cheese ravioli, Cajun-style fresh fish, ginger chicken and teriyaki steak. Touristy but appealing. Prices are deluxe.

The **Discovery Room** (2605 Kaanapali Parkway; 661-0031), located on the eighth floor of the Sheraton Maui, is a spacious lava-walled dining room with a nautical motif and offering views of Kaanapali. Join the line at the buffet table or choose from a menu that includes filet mignon, grilled lamb chops, Polynesian lemon chicken and shrimp scampi. Tabbed in the deluxe range.

North Beach Grille (104 Kaanapali Shores Place, Kaanapali; 661-2000) at the Embassy Suites Resort specializes in American cuisine with a Hawaiian touch. At this pond-rimmed atrium restaurant guests relax in wicker chairs and gaze into an open-view kitchen. Here the chef prepares St. Louis baby back ribs marinated in mango and orange sauce, fresh mahimahi in a beurre blanc sauce, and fire-roasted prime rib rubbed with Hawaiian sea salt. Deluxe to ultra-deluxe.

Beachcomber (2780 Kekaa Drive, Kaanapali; 661-3611), a dinner-only dining room at the Royal Lahaina Resort, has a menu that covers the entire Pacific Rim. You'll find wicker chairs, shell lamps, decorative fans and dragons' heads providing the atmosphere. Add to these features a price structure in the moderate range and you have one of Kaanapali's better values.

If **Lokelani** (100 Nohea Kai Drive, Kaanapali; 667-1200) were located on a trendy corner in Lahaina, there's no doubt that this fresh-fish house would have people lined up waiting for a table. Instead, you'll find it in the Maui Marriott serving specialties such as pan-seared *opaka-*

PUPU GRANDE

*When locals are lining up at a resort hotel's pupu (hors d'ouvres) bar, you know something is up. That's the scene at the Maui Marriott's **Makai Bar** (100 Nohea Kai Drive; 667-1200) where the in crowd gorges on generous portions of sashimi, smoked marlin and ceviche. These dishes, together with nightly specials, make it possible to fashion an entire dinner from these tidbits while enjoying the music and enticing waterfront views.*

paka marinated in *ponzu* then sautéed with lemongrass or seafood ragout prepared with fresh shrimp, scallops, and Hawaiian lobster. Other favorites include rack of lamb over shiitake mushrooms and salad of Kula greens and Roma tomatoes with fried Maui onions. Ask for an outside table overlooking the herb garden where you can enjoy the fresh flowers that add to the tropical ambience. Deluxe to ultra-deluxe.

A traditional Japanese restaurant featuring tableside teppanyaki cooking, **Nikko Japanese Steak House** (100 Nohea Kai Drive, Kaanapali; 667-1200) serves filet mignon, chicken, shrimp, lobster and a vegetarian stir-fry. You can also enjoy sushi, tempura dishes, scallops and fresh fish in the dining room. This Maui Marriott facility is decorated with Japanese woodblock prints and offers booth and table seating. Deluxe.

One of Maui's prettiest restaurants, **Sound of the Falls** (Kaanapali Parkway, Kaanapali; 667-2525) is the plush Westin Maui Hotel's signature dining room. Specializing in sunsets and French-with-a-touch-of-Asia cuisine, it sits beside tumbling waterfalls and gazes out on Lanai. Open for dinner and Sunday brunch, this is the place for vegetable-wrapped Alaskan salmon and egg-battered Pacific abalone. Closed Thursday; prices are ultra-deluxe.

From the ship's rigging, captain's chairs and marlin trophies, you could never guess what they serve at **Erik's Seafood Broiler** (4242 Lower Honoapiilani Road, Kahana; 669-4806). What a surprise to discover a menu stuffed with crabmeat-stuffed prawns, lobster-stuffed chicken breast, Hawaiian salmon and wahoo. The early-bird specials are moderate in price; later in the evening the tab is deluxe.

Dollie's Pub and Café (4310 Lower Honoapiilani Road, Kahana; 669-0266) offers lasagna, fettucine alfredo, chicken marinara, pizza and sandwiches at budget prices. This is a sports-on-the-television bar with a small kitchen and dining room adjacent; noisy but inexpensive.

There's not much of an ocean view at **Kahana Keyes Restaurant** (4327 Lower Honoapiilani Road, Kahana; 669-8071), but you will find a moderately priced menu and wood-trimmed dining room. The bill of fare is pretty standard—steak and seafood; and the decor is comforting if uninspired. Check out the early-bird specials from 5 to 7 p.m.

One of Maui's leading restaurants, **Roy's Kahana Bar and Grill** (4405 Honoapiilani Highway, Kahana; 669-9999) eschews the waterfalls, swans, tinkling pianists and other accoutrements of the island's top dining rooms. Instead, this spacious second-story establishment looks like a gallery with its exposed-beam ceiling, track lighting and Hawaiian paintings. The open kitchen serves up such gourmet creations as *opaka-paka* with macadamia nut and lobster butter, Mongolian loin of lamb with lemongrass, smoked swordfish with salsa, *imu*-roasted pork, and blackened ahi with soy-mustard butter. Deluxe to ultra-deluxe. Reservations are a must!

Crazy for chocolates? Stop at the Hyatt Regency Maui's Lahaina Provision Company. The all-you-can-eat Chocoholic Bar will satisfy even the wildest cravings.

A few steps away, Roy Yamaguchi, the owner of the Kahana Bar and Grill, has created a sister establishment, **R.J.'s Ranch House** (4405 Honoapiilani Highway, Kahana; 669-5000). Pine floors, ranch murals, and sculptures of cows and pigs create a Hawaiian *paniolo* motif. The moderate-priced entrées complete the theme: Yankee pot roast, southern-fried chicken, spicy coyote wings, deep-fried white fish with crisp hush puppies and a sloppy chili cheeseburger with grilled onions.

For Mongolian beef, Peking duck or hot Szechuan bean curd, try **China Boat** (4474 Lower Honoapiilani Road, Kahana; 669-5089). At this family-style restaurant, you can ease into a lacquered seat and take in the Japanese *ukiyoe* prints that adorn the place. Adding to the ambience are lava walls that showcase beautiful Chinese ceramic pieces. Patio dining is also available. Moderate.

At the **Orient Express** (5315 Lower Honoapiilani Road, Napili; 669-8077), they feature a variety of Thai and Chinese dishes including shrimp saté, clay-pot seafood dishes, sour shrimp soup, red curry beef, and Thai noodles stir-fried with pork, egg and crushed peanuts. Part of the Napili Shores Resort, this lava-walled restaurant has a shocking-pink-and-purple color scheme. Moderate.

Maui aficionados agree that **The Plantation House Restaurant** (2000 Plantation Club Drive, Kahana; 669-6299) is among the island's best. Capturing their accolades is a spacious establishment with panoramic views of the Kapalua region and a decor that mixes mahogany and wicker with orchids and a roaring fire. Not to be upstaged by the surroundings, the chef wok-fries jumbo prawns with Maui onions and prepares a mixed grill of lamb chops, blackened fresh fish and curried chicken sausage. For lighter appetites there are Nicoise salads, honey guava scallops, and a wide range of soups and sandwiches. Deluxe to ultra-deluxe.

There's little doubt that Hawaii's finest sunsets occur off the southwest coast of Maui. One of the best spots to catch the spectacle is **The Bay Club** (1 Bay Drive, Kapalua; 669-5656) at the Kapalua Bay Hotel, an oceanfront dining room that looks out on Molokai and Lanai. More than just a feast for the eyes, this open-air restaurant offers a gourmet menu at lunch and dinner. You can watch the sky melt from deep blue to flaming red while dining on bouillabaisse, scallops with capers, Pacific lobster tail, broiled lamb chops or filet mignon. A rough life indeed. Dress code: no shorts, jeans or T-shirts; ultra-deluxe.

For something less expensive, consider **The Market Café** (1 Bay Drive, Kapalua; 669-4888). It's located in the Kapalua Shops adjacent to the

Kapalua Bay Hotel and shares its space with a gourmet market. Comfortably equipped with wooden booths and bentwood chairs, the dining area presents fresh fish, steak teriyaki, chicken tetrazini and several other Italian specialties at moderate prices. They also serve very inexpensive breakfasts and lunches.

Following the "when in Rome" adage, the Ritz-Carlton Kapalua has dedicated its signature restaurant to the fine art of Hawaiian cuisine. At **The Grill** (1 Ritz-Carlton Drive, Kapalua; 669-6200) you can expect fresh ono in passion-fruit sauce, seared prawns, and beef tenderloin in chili ginger sauce. The dimly lit dining room has a formal clublike atmosphere. Outside its three glass walls are panoramic views of Oneloa Bay and the hotel's golf course. Patio dining is also available. Ultra-deluxe.

For a less formal venue in the Ritz-Carlton, consider the Pacific Rim cuisine at **The Terrace**. Rattan chairs and teak tables add a graceful note to this poolside dining room. Try the wok-seared ahi tuna, duck with ginger and plum sauce, pizza with spicy Thai prawns, spinach salad, or lobster pot-stickers. Moderate to deluxe.

KAANAPALI-KAPALUA AREA SHOPPING

Worthy of mention is **Whalers Village** in the Kaanapali Beach Resort on Route 30. This sprawling complex combines a shopping mall with an outdoor museum. Numbered among the stores you'll find gift emporia featuring coral and shells, a shirt store with wild island designs, other stores offering fine men's and women's fashions and a **Waldenbooks** (661-8638) bookstore.

Several shops in this split-level complex should not be missed. **The Secret Jungle** (661-8651) specializes in the cloisonné jewelry and silk-screened fabrics of Laurel Burch. Around the corner at **Lahaina Print-sellers Ltd.** (667-7617), they purvey "fine antique maps and prints,"

SCRIMSHAW TREASURES

*Perhaps the best place in Whaler's Village to discover the whaling tradition is **Lahaina Scrimshaw** (661-4034). During their long journeys, sailors once whiled away the hours by etching and engraving on ivory, creating beautiful articles of scrimshaw. The sale of ivory from animals taken by hunters is banned, but the fossilized remains of ancient mammoths and walruses have kept this art alive. Using ivory that is thousands of years old, artists create a wide array of functional and decorative pieces, many of which are traded by aficionados of this art form.*

while at **Blue Ginger Designs** (667-5793) original styles in women's and children's clothing are featured.

Silks Kaanapali (667-7133) is the place to find hand-painted silk and rayon dresses and sarongs. Belts, hats, jewelry and other accessories are also sold here.

Another store worth visiting here is **Endangered Species** (661-1114), a preservationist shop selling photos, sculptures, and paintings of sharks, whales, and rainforests. Through sales of these products it also helps support many environmental causes.

And then, to help make shopping the grand adventure it should be, there are the displays. Within this mazework mall you'll discover blunderbusses, intricate scrimshaw pieces, the skeletal remains of leviathans and whaling boats with iron harpoons splayed from the bow. Practically everything, in fact, that a whaler (or a cruising shopper) could desire.

Ever wonder where travel writers shop for kitsch? Members of that dissolute group have been known to frequent **O'Rourke's Tourist Trap** (4405 Lower Honoapiiilani Highway, Kahana; 669-1406). Here under one large roof are glass pineapples, gecko pins, plastic leis, cultured coral pieces and hundreds of other mementos of the islands.

For serious shoppers, ready to spend money or be damned, there is nothing to compare with the neighboring hotels. Set like gems within this tourist cluster are several world-class hotels, each hosting numerous elegant shops.

Foremost is the **Hyatt Regency Maui**, along whose wood-paneled lobby are stores that might well be deemed mini-museums. One shop contains exquisite pieces of hand-chiseled crystal. Another, called **Elephant Walk** (667-2848), displays *koa* wood furniture, baskets and Niihau shell jewelry. There are art galleries, fabric shops, candy stores, a

---

PUEONE O HONOKAHUA

The Kapalua area includes one of Maui's most important cultural zones, Pueone O Honokahua. This 14-acre preserve, near the Ritz-Carlton Kapalua, was the site of fishing shrines and heiaus where the ancient Hawaiians worshipped their gods and made astronomical observations. Today you can see a burial ground dating back to 950 A.D. and portions of the King's Highway, a 16th-century stone road around Maui. Also extant are the outlines of terraced taro patches farmed by early inhabitants. Although this land has been claimed in turn by King Kamehameha III, the sugar king, H. P. Baldwin, and lastly the Maui Land and Pineapple Company, the state now protects and preserves it as a native Hawaiian sanctuary.

In old Hawaii, Kaanapali was a retreat for Maui royalty.

luggage shop and more—set in an open-air lobby that is filled with rare statuary and exotic birds.

A favorite West Maui shop is **Rhonda's Quilts** (200 Nohea Kai Drive, Kaanapali; 661-1234), where you'll find wall hangings, Thai silk pillows and needlepoint supplies as well as an array of quilts. Many of the quilts are designed by local artists.

La Bareda (100 Nohea Kai Drive, Kaanapali; 667-8226) is an excellent place to find inexpensive Hawaiian souvenirs such as sarongs, straw hats, jewelry and T-shirts. This shop in the Maui Marriott hotel is also knee-deep in key chains, pennants and ceramic pineapples.

The **Circle Gallery** (2365 Kaanapali Parkway, Kaanapali; 667-0355) features a wide range of contemporary abstract art and original animated pieces from Walt Disney and Hanna-Barbera cartoons. The shop's art-to-wear collection is highlighted by graphics by Erté that have been transformed into jewelry.

The shopping annex at the **Kapalua Bay Hotel** (1 Bay Drive, Kapalua) is another upscale address. Among the temptations is **Mandalay** (669-6170), specializing in silks and cottons from Asia. There are blouses and jackets for women as well as a small collection of artfully crafted jewelry. Also stop by **South Seas of Kapalua** (669-1249), which has native masks from New Guinea and other artwork from Oceania.

If you're traveling with young ones or looking for a souvenir for those you left behind, stop by **Kapalua Kids** (669-0033). Here you can buy children's books on Hawaii as well as soft toys and an array of clothing.

At the **Plantation Course Golf Shop** (2000 Plantation Club Drive, Kapalua; 669-8877) you'll find an impressive collection of jackets, shirts, sweaters, sweatshirts and shorts, many with a tropical flair. This is also a good place to look for the work of signature designers.

KAANAPALI-KAPALUA AREA NIGHTLIFE

A solo pianist performs nightly at the Hyatt Regency Maui's elegant waterfront **Swan Court** (200 Nohea Kai Drive; 661-1234). For Hawaiian music, head over to the **Weeping Banyan**, an open-air lounge.

There's music and Hawaiian entertainment at the Westin Maui's **Villa Terrace** (2365 Kaanapali Parkway, Kaanapali; 667-2525). At the hotel's **Sound of the Falls**, a classical pianist plays nightly.

At the Maui Marriott (667-1200), the **Makai Bar** cooks every night with a duo or trio performing Hawaiian and Pop numbers. If you'd rather get up there and perform yourself, you can join the hostess in a

Where the royal Kaanapali Golf Course sits, Hawaiian royalty played the ancient game of ulu maika, a form of lawn bowling played with heavy balls of lava.

karaoke-style sing-along at the **Lobby Bar** on Thursday, Friday or Saturday. On Sunday night a stand-up comedian will take your place.

Possibly the prettiest place in these parts to enjoy a late night drink beneath the tropic moon is **El Crab Catcher** (661-4423). Located in the Whalers Village mall, this club features contemporary Hawaiian music on Friday and Saturday nights. The place is located right on the water, so you can listen to a slow set, then stroll the beach.

The Sheraton Maui (Kaanapali Parkway; 661-0031) is a prime nightspot both early and later in the evening. Just before sunset you can watch the torchlighting and cliff-diving ceremony from the **Sundowner Bar**. Then adjourn to **On The Rocks** for their karaoke program.

There's Hawaiian-style entertainment nightly at the **Royal Ocean Terrace Lounge** (2780 Kekaa Drive, Kaanapali; 661-3611), a beachfront watering hole on the grounds of the Royal Lahaina Resort. Arrive early and you can watch the sunset between Lanai and Molokai followed by the ubiquitous torch-lighting ceremony.

A guitar soloist plays contemporary tunes at the thatch-roofed **Ohana Bar and Grill** (104 Kaanapali Shores Place, Kaanapali; 661-2000). This open-air establishment, its furniture creatively designed with a clam-shell motif, is a favorite among sunset watchers.

For something entirely different, call the Royal Lahaina Resort and make reservations for **Suspects Murder Mystery Dinner Theater** (2780 Kekaa Drive, Kaanapali; 661-3611). The show—which runs on Thursday, Friday and Saturday night—offers guests a buffet-style dinner with standard steak, chicken and fish entrées. Also on the menu is a murder and a cast of actors trying to find the guilty party. The show takes about four hours and its one all-inclusive price is ultra-deluxe.

For soft entertainment in a relaxed setting, try the **Bay Club** (669-8008) at the Kapalua Bay Hotel. This open-air lounge with nightly pianist is set in a lovely restaurant overlooking the water. The melodies are as serene and relaxing as the views of neighboring Molokai.

In the Kapalua Bay Hotel lobby, a soloist performs easy listening tunes in **The Bay Lounge** where you can enjoy *pupus* and great views of the Pacific. There's also a Hawaiian trio and hula show nightly at the **Pool Terrace**.

A solo Hawaiian guitarist plays in the evenings at **The Lobby Lounge and Library** (1 Ritz-Carlton Drive, Kapalua; 669-6200). The Ritz-Carlton Kapalua also features Hawaiian dancing and music in the **Terrace Restaurant**. At the **Sunset Lounge** you can enjoy a pianist and vocalist.

KAANAPALI-KAPALUA AREA BEACHES AND PARKS

Kaanapali Resort Beaches: The sprawling complex of Kaanapali hotels sits astride a beautiful white-sand beach that extends for three miles. Looking out on Lanai and Molokai, this is a classic palm-fringed strand. The entire area is heavily developed and crowded with tourists glistening in coconut oil. But it is an extraordinarily fine beach where the swimming is very good and the skindiving excellent around Black Rock at the Sheraton Maui. To get there, take the public right-of-way to the beach from any of the Kaanapali resort hotels. The beach has no facilities, but there are restaurants nearby.

Compared to the beaches fronting Kaanapali's nearby resorts, **Honokowai Beach Park** is a bit disappointing. The large lawn is pleasant enough, but the beach itself is small, with a reef that projects right to the shoreline. On the other hand, the view of Molokai is awesome. The beach is on Lower Honoapiilani Road (which is the oceanfront section of Route 30) north of Kaanapali in Honokowai. In the shallow reef waters the swimming and snorkeling are fair; surfing is nonexistent. Threadfin and *ulua* are among the most frequent catches. Picnic tables, restrooms and showers are available and directly across the street is a supermarket.

Condominiums run wall-to-wall along the small cove that is **Napili Bay.** The crowded but beautiful white-sand beach studded with palm trees and looking out on Molokai is several miles north of Kaanapali, with rights-of-way to the beach from Lower Honoapiilani Road via Napili Place or Hui Drive. Swimming and snorkeling are delightful and the surfing here is particularly delightful for beginners.

Kapalua Beach, the next cove over from Napili Bay, is equally beautiful, but not as heavily developed. The crescent of white sand that lines Kapalua Bay is bounded on either end by rocky points and backdropped by a line of coconut trees and the Kapalua Bay Hotel. There's a right-of-way to the beach from Lower Honoapiilani Road near the Napili Kai Beach Club. Swimming and snorkeling are excellent.

One of Maui's nicest beach parks is the **D. T. Fleming Park.** It has a spacious white-sand beach and a rolling lawn shaded with palm and ironwood trees. Unfortunately, a major resort resides just uphill from the beach. Sometimes windy, the park is plagued by rough and dangerous surf during the winter. Use caution! There's a nice view of Molokai's rugged East End. Located just off Honoapiilani Highway, about seven miles north of Kaanapali, D. T. Fleming Park has restrooms, a picnic area and showers. You'll find good swimming and bodysurfing and fair snorkeling here. There are also good breaks nearby at Little Makaha, named after the famous Oahu beach. For anglers the prime catches here are *ulua* and *papio*.

It was from the shoreline near Kahakuloa that the Polynesian canoe Hokulea *left on its famous voyage.*

Northwest Maui

To escape from the crowds and commotion of the Kaanapali-Kapalua area and travel north on the Honoapiilani Highway is to journey from the ridiculous to the sublime. As you curve along the edge of the West Maui Mountains, en route around the side of the island to Kahului and Wailuku, you'll pass several hidden beaches that lie along an exotic and undeveloped shore. This is a region of the Valley Isle rarely ever seen by visitors.

Near the rocky beach and lush valley at **Honokohau Bay**, the Honoapiilani Highway (Route 30) becomes the Kahekili Highway (Route 340). This macadam track snakes high above the ocean, hugging the coastline. From the highway rises a series of multihued **sandstone cliffs** that seem alien to this volcanic region and create a picturesque backdrop to the rocky shore.

After several miles, the road turns to dirt and soon deteriorates into a bone-jangling series of ruts punctuated with potholes. The scenery is some of the most magnificent on Maui. About a mile down the dirt road sits the rustic village of **Kahakuloa**. Nestled in an overgrown valley beside a deep blue bay, the community is protected by a solitary headland rising directly from the sea. Woodframe houses and churches, which appear ready to fall to the next gusting wind, are spotted throughout this enchanting area. Kahakuloa is cattle country, and you'll find that the villagers live and farm much as their forefathers did back when most of Maui was unclaimed terrain.

The road ascends again and improves somewhat outside Kahakuloa. Opening below you, one valley after another falls seaward in a series of spine-backed ridges. Above the road, the mountain range rises toward its 5788-foot summit at Puu Kukui.

There are lush gulches farther along as the road returns to pavement and descends into the plantation town of **Waihee**. Here cane fields, dotted with small farm houses, slope from the roadside up to the foothills of the West Maui Mountains.

You're still on the Kahekili Highway, but now once again it really is a highway, a well-paved road that leads toward Kahului. Located just northwest of town a side road leads to two sacred spots. The first, **Halekii Heiau**, overlooking Kahului Bay and Iao Stream, dates from the

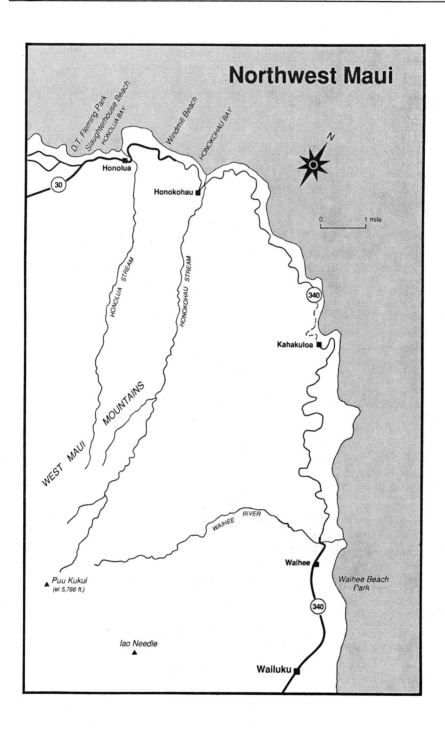

1700s. Today this temple, once as large as a football field, is little more than a stone heap. **Pihana Kalani Heiau**, a short distance away, was once a sacrificial temple.

Before driving this route, as well as the back road from Hana to Ulupalakua, remember that the car rental agencies will not insure you over these rugged tracks. Many folks cover the roads anyway, and I highly recommend that you explore them both if weather permits.

NORTHWEST MAUI BEACHES AND PARKS

Mokuleia Beach or **Slaughterhouse Beach** is a lovely patch of white sand bounded by cliffs and looking out on Molokai. Set at the end of a shallow cove, the beach is partially protected. To get there, take Honoapiilani Highway (Route 30) for exactly eight-tenths of a mile past D. T. Fleming Park. A steep path leads down about 100 yards from the parking area to the beach. Swimming, snorkeling and surfing are all good. This is part of a marine sanctuary so fishing is not permitted. There are no facilities here.

A rocky beach makes the cliff-rimmed **Honolua Bay** unappealing for sunbathers, but there are rich coral deposits offshore and beautiful trees growing near the water. To reach it, take Honoapiilani Highway (Route 30) for about one-and-a-third miles north from D. T. Fleming Park. The dirt road to the beach is open only to cars with boats in tow. Park with the other cars along Route 30 and follow the paths to the beach. In winter you're likely to find crowds along the top of the cliff watching surfers work some of the finest breaks in all Hawaii: perfect tubes up to 15 feet. Swimming is good, but the bottom is rocky. Snorkeling is excellent, particularly on the west side of the bay. No fishing is allowed; this is part of a marine sanctuary. There are no facilities (and usually very few people) here.

A white-sand beach studded with rocks, **Punalau** or **Windmill Beach** is surrounded by cliffs and intriguing rock formations. Very secluded, it is just three-and-a-half miles north from D. T. Fleming Park on Honoapiilani Highway (Route 30). Turn left onto the dirt road and follow it a short distance to the beach. The swimming is okay and when the water is calm snorkeling is excellent. A fascinating reef extends along the coast all through this area. Surfing is fine, peaking in winter; left and right slides. Leatherback, papio, milkfish, moano and big-eyed scad are the primary catches for anglers. For those interested in pitching a camp here, a permit is required from Maui Pineapple Co., Honolua Division, 4900 Honoapiilani Highway, Lahaina (669-6201) and must be obtained in person. There is no charge, but there is a three-day limit. Nor are there any facilities.

The rocky beach on **Honokohau Bay** is surrounded by cliffs. To the interior, a lush valley rises steadily into the folds of the West Maui Mountains. To get there, follow Honoapiilani Highway (Route 30) about six miles north of D. T. Fleming Park. When the water is calm, swimming and snorkeling are good. The surf offers rugged, two- to twelve-foot breaks. Keep in mind the changeable nature of this wave action, since it can vary quickly from the gentle to the dangerous. Milkfish, *papio*, leatherback, *moano* and big-eyed scad are the principal species caught in these waters. Camping is allowed here, but the place is very rocky, and there are no facilities.

SIX

Kihei-Wailea Area

Stretching from Maalaea Bay to Makena is a nearly continuous succession of beautiful beaches that make Kihei and Wailea favored resort destinations. Second only to the Lahaina—Kaanapali area in popularity, this seaside enclave rests in the rainshadow of Haleakala, which looms in the background. Maui's southeastern shore receives only ten inches of rain a year, making it the driest, sunniest spot on the island. It also experiences heavy winds, particularly in the afternoon, which sweep across the island's isthmus.

Since the 1970s, this long, lean stretch of coast has become a developer's playground. Kihei in particular, lacking a master plan, has grown by accretion from a small local community into a haphazard collection of condominiums and mini-malls. It's an unattractive, six-mile strip lined by a golden beach.

Situated strategically along this beachfront are cement **pillboxes**, reminders of World War II's threatened Japanese invasion. Placed along Kihei Road just north of town, they are not far from **Kealia Pond Bird Sanctuary**, a 300-acre reserve frequented by migratory waterfowl as well as Hawaiian stilts and Hawaiian coots.

To the south lies Wailea, an urbane answer to the random growth patterns of its scruffy neighbor. Wailea is a planned resort, all 1450 manicured acres of it. Here *kiawe* scrubland has been transformed into a flowering oasis that is home to five top-class hotels and six condominiums, as well as the required retinue of golf courses, tennis courts and overpriced shops. Like Kihei, it is blessed with beautiful beaches.

Home to some of Maui's most luxurious resorts, Wailea is the place to find Picasso originals, 50,000-square-foot spas and villas designed to keep a smile on the face of a high roller. Mediterranean- and plantation-style architecture, accented by polished limestone tile and granite boulders imported from Mount Fuji, make this swank resort area an international retreat.

If your definition of a good vacation includes five crescent beaches, oceanfront links, vintage champagne and 24-hour room service, you have arrived. Connected by a mile-and-a-half-long ocean walk, the resort's luxury properties comprise a self-contained retreat. Spread across a region three times the size of Waikiki, Wailea is the Valley Isle's fastest growing resort destination.

You'll have to go well past Wailea, to where the coast road becomes a dirt track, to escape the tourist complexes. I highly recommend visiting **Makena Beach**, located along Makena Alanui Road about four miles beyond Wailea. Although development has struck here, too, Makena is still one of Maui's finest strands. A hippie hangout in the 1960s and early 1970s, it still retains a freewheeling atmosphere, especially at nearby "Little Makena," Maui's most famous nude beach.

Past here the road gets rough as it presses south to **Ahihi-Kinau Reserve**. Encompassing over 2000 acres of land and ocean bottom, this preserve harbors an amazing array of marine life and contains the remains of an early Hawaiian fishing village. Almost 100 larval fish species and about two dozen species of stony coral have been found in this ecologically rich reserve.

The road continues on, bisecting the **1790 lava flow**, which resulted from Haleakala's last eruption. The flow created Cape Kinau, a thumb-shaped peninsula dividing Ahihi Bay and **La Perouse Bay**. When I drove this route recently in a compact rental car, I reached La Perouse Bay before being forced by poor road conditions to turn back. The bay is named for the ill-starred French navigator, Jean-François de Galaup La Pérouse, who anchored here in 1786, the first Westerner to visit Maui. After a brief sojourn in this enchanting spot, he sailed off and was later lost at sea.

KIHEI-WAILEA AREA LODGING

Like Kaanapali, this oceanfront strip features condominiums, but there are a couple of moderately priced hotels. The **Nona Lani Cottages** (455 South Kihei Road, Kihei; 879-2497) tops the list, with eight quaint wooden cottages situated across busy Kihei Road from a white-sand beach. Each is a one-bedroom unit with lanai, all-electric kitchen and a living room capable of housing two extra sleepers. There's wall-to-wall carpeting and a shower-tub combination, plus television, but no phone or air conditioner. Like most cottages in Hawaii, these are extremely popular, so you'll need to reserve them far in advance. There is a four-

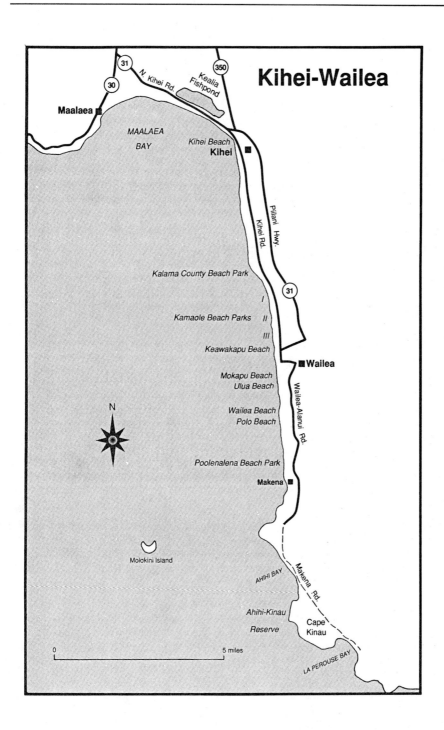

Score a hole in one at the Maui Inter-Continental's weekly chipping contest and you'll get a free room for three nights.

---

night minimum from April 1 to December 15; seven–night minimum from December 16 to March 31.

Spread across 28 acres, the **Maui Lu Resort** (575 South Kihei Road, Kihei; 879-5881) is tropically landscaped with palm trees and flowering plants. Within the grounds, which are across the street from a beach, you'll find a pool, two tennis courts and a huge restaurant. The guest rooms are furnished in standard fashion and located in a series of interconnecting buildings with some accommodations on the beach. Moderate to deluxe.

Down the road at the **Wailea Oceanfront Hotel** (2980 South Kihei Road, Kihei; 879-7744) you'll find a series of six buildings designed in mock-Hawaiian style and sandwiched between the highway and a white-sand beach. Here a moderate-to-deluxe tab books a tiny, attractively decorated room with carpeting, air conditioning, television and refrigerator.

On Mokapu Beach, set on 15-acres of tropical gardens, **Stouffer's Wailea Beach Resort** (3550 Wailea Alanui Drive, Wailea; 879-4900) offers 347 rooms and suites furnished with rattan, wicker and cane furniture. The contemporary Hawaiian decor features striped sofas, quilted pillow covers and tropical foliage. Some oceanfront units come with telescopes perfect for whale watching. Other amenities include complimentary Japanese *hapi* coats, free first-run movies, double vanities and lanais with comfortable chaise longues. Ultra-deluxe.

Entered via a porte cochère, the **Maui Inter-Continental Resort** (3700 Wailea Alanui Drive, Wailea; 879-1922) welcomes visitors with an impressive Pacific Rim art collection. The nicest attribute of this 22-acre complex is, however, its open design. You'll find meandering paths that lead past manicured gardens down to a sandy beach. Most of the 516 low-rise and tower rooms come with ocean views and have wicker furniture, spacious lanais and contemporary artwork. There's also an outstanding family plan that provides a second room free for the children of parents who reserve a room at the regular rate. Ultra-deluxe.

One of the world's richest men invested $600 million to create the **Grand Wailea Resort Hotel and Spa** (3850 Wailea Alanui Drive, Wailea; 875-1234). From Fernando Botero's whimsical full-figured sculptures in the lobby to the swimming pool modeled after William Randolph Hearst's imperial plunge at San Simeon, the results are grandiose. Here you can get married in a New England–style chapel, see the collection of 250 lithographs by Picasso, or ride the world's only water elevator to the top of a waterslide that plunges into a "canyon riverpool." All 787 ocean-front rooms and suites are built around an open-air atrium. These spacious accommodations have king-sized beds, luxurious sofas, Hawaiian prints and marble baths. Workaholics will be relieved to learn that attendants at Grand Wailea provide complimentary laptop computers to the guests at the pool. For those interested, there's the spa, a lavish two-story gold and marble complex that offers European and Hawaiian treatments. An ultra-deluxe resort for the rich and famous, or those who would like to mingle with them.

The lushly landscaped **Four Seasons Resort Wailea** (3900 Wailea Alanui Drive, Wailea; 874-8000) is the ultimate among ultimate destinations. The only Maui resort we know to feature a trompe l'oeil artwork in the lobby, it's a windswept, neo-Georgian-style complex set on a luxurious beach. Furnished with wicker and rattan, most of the 452 plantation-style rooms offer ocean views. Casablanca fans, tropical plants and marbletop vanities add to the comfort of this ultra-deluxe-priced hotel. Louvered doors open onto spacious lanais. Reflecting pools, waterfalls and fountains give the public areas an elegant tropical air.

The all-suite **Kea Lani Hotel** (4100 Wailea Alanui Drive, Wailea; 875-4100) is a 22-acre resort done in southern Mediterranean style. Turning its back on Hawaiian royalty, the Eurocentric lobby would look familiar to Louis XIV. Seven waterfalls, four fountains and several swim-up bars create attractions decadent enough for the Sun King himself. Among the accommodations are 413 suites and 37 oceanfront villas, each appointed with oak fixtures, floral prints and mirrored doors. The Roman-style baths feature Italian marble (of course) and the two-story villa comes with its own plunge pool. Ultra-deluxe.

Its remote location makes the **Maui Prince Hotel** (5400 Makena Alanui Drive, Makena; 874-1111) an unusual find. Built around a courtyard adorned with lush tropical gardens and lily ponds, the 310-room establishment rewards those willing to drive a few extra minutes to Maui's southernmost retreat. Here you're likely to be lulled to sleep by the sound of the surf and awakened by a crowing rooster. Decorated with

---

UNDER THE VOLCANO

Hawaii's newest volcano is right next to the Grand Wailea's Canyon Action Pool. It stands a mere 34 feet high, but don't be deceived. This active firepit rumbles and vents steam as predictably as Old Faithful does. Sound intimidating? Not to worry: Tucked beneath this geological wonder, you'll discover the Volcano Bar serving tropical drinks, sandwiches and pupus.

---

*Free overnight sandal repair is offered to all guests at the Four Seasons Resort
Wailea. Now that's service!*

---

heliconia and bougainvillea, the rooms and suites open onto lanais. This
V-shaped hotel is next door to two of Maui's top golf courses. Tabbed in
the ultra-deluxe range.

KIHEI-WAILEA AREA CONDOMINIUMS

Leilani Kai (1226 Uluniu Street, Kihei; 879-2606). This cozy nine-
unit apartment hotel is right on the beach. Studio apartments are $75
double ($60 during the off-season, May 1 to November 30); one-bedroom
units are $100 double ($75 off-season); two bedrooms will run you $125
for one to four people ($90 off-season).

Kihei Kai (61 North Kihei Road, Kihei; 879-2357). Oceanside one-
bedroom apartments are $70 to $95 double ($55 to $80 from mid-April
to mid-December; each has television, full kitchen and lanai).

Sunseeker Resort (551 South Kihei Road, Kihei; 879-1261). A small,
personalized place where studios with kitchenettes go for $50 double,
one-bedrooms $60 double and two-bedrooms $80 for four people. Add
$6 for each additional person.

Mana Kai–Maui Apartment Hotel (2960 South Kihei Road, Kihei; 879-1561). This highrise condominium has "hotel units" that con-
sist of the extra bedroom and bath from a two-bedroom apartment,
renting for $90 ($95 from December 17 through April 15). One-bedroom
units with kitchens start at $155 ($175 in winter). The condo has a beachfront location, plus an adjoining restaurant and bar.

Lihi Kai (2121 Iliili Road, Kihei; 879-2335). This establishment has
nine beach cottages with full kitchens, all renting for $59 single or dou-
ble. Rates are lower for a seven-night stay. To be sure of getting a
cottage, you'd best make reservations far in advance. There is a three-
night minimum.

Kamaole Beach Royale (2385 South Kihei Road, Kihei; 879-3131).
A six-story condo across the street from a beach park, this has one-bedroom
apartments for $65 double; two-bedroom units, $75 double. From December to April, the rates increase to $90 and $100, respectively.

Kapulanikai (73 Kapu Place, Kihei; 879-1607). A cozy place with
only 12 apartments, all of which overlook the ocean and a grassy, park-
like setting. One-bedroom apartments rent for $80 single or double ($65
from April to mid-December).

KIHEI-WAILEA AREA RESTAURANTS

Now that condominiums have mushroomed from its white sands, Kihei is no longer a poor person's paradise. Yet there are still several short-order griddles like **Suda's Snack Shop** (61 South Kihei Road, Kihei; 879-2668) around.

You'll find another take-out window at **Azeka's Market Snack Shop** (1278 South Kihei Road; 879-0611) in nearby Azeka Place Shopping Center. For atmosphere there's a parking lot, but for food there's a fair choice, with hamburgers and plate lunches priced low. Both are priced in the budget range.

Surfside Spirits and Deli (1993 South Kihei Road, Kihei; 879-1385) has a take-out delicatessen serving sandwiches, salads and slaw. Budget.

At **Canton Chef** (2463 South Kihei Road, Kihei; 879-1988), on the other hand, the cuisine ranges from roast duck to beef with oyster sauce. This traditional Chinese restaurant offers almost 100 different choices including a selection of spicy Szechuan dishes. Budget to moderate.

For a relaxed meal, I like **Luigi's Pasta & Pizzeria** (Azeka Place Shopping Center, 1280 South Kihei Road, Kihei; 879-4446). Built on three levels and decorated in a nautical motif, it has a comfortable laid-back atmosphere. The menu consists of Italian dishes like chicken parmesan and fettuccine alfredo as well as shrimp and steak platters. A gathering place for local residents, Luigi's is easygoing and friendly. Dinner only; moderate prices.

BACKWARDS LUNCH IN KEIKI HEAVEN

Wailea, where all the major resorts offer special programs for younger guests, is heaven for kids—and for parents who need a little time off! These upscale hotels provide an opportunity for your children to meet kids from around the world, as well as have a fun-filled day at the beach. Stouffer Wailea Beach Resort's **Camp Wailea** *explores the island's geology and marine life with field trips to lava flows and coral reefs.* **Club Gecko** *(Club Gecko?) at Maui Inter-Continental Resort emphasizes arts and crafts. At the Grand Wailea Resort and Spa, the 20,000-square-foot* **Camp Grande** *includes a computer learning center, kids' pool, and classes on local culture and ecology. The Escapades Restaurant even serves a "backwards lunch" that begins with dessert and ends with an appetizer. Four Seasons Resort Wailea introduces five- to twelve-year-olds to the fine arts of hula dancing, kite making and volcano building. At the Kea Lani Hotel, children have a chance to explore tide pools, weave palm fronds and talk story. Similarly, the Maui Prince Hotel* **Kid's Club** *offers sandcastle building, bamboo pole fishing and nature hikes. Check with the concierge at the above hotels for schedule and fee information.*

Margarita's Beach Cantina (101 North Kihei Road, Kihei; 879-5311) is one of those big brassy Mexican restaurants that are ever more present along the beaches. The kind that have live sports on big-screen television and a buzzing night scene. What sells this place is the ocean-side dining and happy-hour margarita specials. The menu covers lunch and dinner, featuring carnitas, tacos and chimichangas, as well as non-Mexican favorites such as steak and pasta, and is moderately priced.

For inexpensive Korean food, there's **The Kal Bi House** (1215 South Kihei Road, Kihei; 874-8454). Squeezed into a corner of Kihei Center and furnished with molded-plastic seats, it's not much on atmosphere. But it's hard to beat their budget-priced barbecued ribs, grilled chicken and beef marinated in Korean sauce, *katsu* chicken, or Korean soups. A good place for a takeout meal.

If you prefer something from Southeast Asia, **Royal Thai Cuisine** (Azeka Place Shopping Center, 1280 South Kihei Road, Kihei; 874-0813) sits across the street in yet another shopping mall. Here the chairs are wood, the menu includes *dozens* of selections, such as crab legs, chili shrimp, cashew chicken or seafood combinations. Budget to moderate.

Did you say Greek? No problem. Just a few malls away (this one is called Kai Nani Village) is the **Greek Bistro** (2511 South Kihei Road, Kihei; 879-9330) with a full selection of Mediterranean dishes such as gyros, moussaka, souvlaki, lamb kebabs and dolmas. These come to you at a moderate price tag.

Or forget the ethnic food and head next door to the **Kihei Prime Rib and Seafood House** (2511 South Kihei Road, Kihei; 879-1954). A reliable if undistinguished dining room, it offers a good salad bar and numerous beef and fresh fish dishes. There are views across the road

---

HULA MOONS

*From the day his ship docked in 1917 until his death four decades later, the writer Don Blanding lured visitors to the islands with more than a dozen books. An exhibition of this haole poet laureate's work is found at the Maui Inter-Continental Resort restaurant named for one of his best-known volumes, **Hula Moons** (3700 Wailea Alanui Drive, Wailea; 879-1922). The open-air establishment is like a small museum appointed with art pieces, ceramic plates and aloha shirts that Blanding designed, as well as his books, poems and sheet music. The menu includes herb-marinated rack of lamb, mixed grill, and a steamed seafood basket with scallops, lobster and crab. Fresh berries in wine sauce with ice cream highlight the dessert list. Deluxe prices.*

overlooking the ocean. Deluxe to ultra-deluxe; there's a moderately priced early-bird special from 5:00 to 6:00 p.m.

The **Longhouse Restaurant** (575 South Kihei Road, Kihei; 879-5881) at the Maui Lu Resort is a cavernous hall with bandstand and sunken dining room. Often you'll be serenaded at dinner by one of the resident musicians. The menu here is a surf-and-turf affair priced in the moderate-to-deluxe range. They also serve breakfast, but the musicians won't join you for your eggs benedict.

Why do celebrities such as Richard Dreyfuss, Harry Hamlin and Debra Winger book reservations at **Carelli's On The Beach** (2980 South Kihei Road, Kihei; 875-0001)? Perhaps it's the imaginative Italian menu at this Keawakapu Beach establishment. Specialties include steamed clams in garlic, interesting pastas, gnocchi with pancetta and fire-roasted rack of lamb. The open-air dining room, with its murals of Venice and the chic Mangia bar, adds to the allure. Deluxe.

All those *Travel/Holiday Magazine* awards at the entrance to **Raffles** (3550 Wailea Alanui Drive, Wailea; 879-4900) signify that this is Stouffer Wailea Resort's signature restaurant and one of the most highly respected dining rooms on the island. With its bamboo drapes and brass chandeliers, the place is a study in British colonial elegance. The cuisine, however, is island classic: rack of lamb with mango chutney, ahi in *wasabi* ginger cream, *ono* with papaya and breast of chicken with Maui onion. The tab naturally is ultra-deluxe. Raffles is open for dinner and Sunday brunch only.

At **Gion Hamasaku** (3550 Wailea Alanui Drive, Wailea; 879-4900) you can choose between tableside *teppanyaki* cooking or a private booth with *shoji* screens. Built in Japan, broken down and shipped to Maui for reassembly, this beautiful restaurant in the Stouffer Wailea Beach Resort was created with the guidance of one of Kyoto's leading restaurant-owning families. Specialties such as tempura, *yosenabe*, *shabu-shabu*, sukiyaki and chicken *mizutaki* are served by kimono-clad waitresses. There's also a popular sushi bar on the premises. Prices here range from deluxe to ultra-deluxe.

One of Maui's finest open-air dining rooms, the tropical **Pacific Grill** (Four Seasons Resort Wailea, 3900 Wailea Alanui Drive, Wailea; 874-8000) has an open-view Asian kitchen. Trade winds and Casablanca-style fans cool the dining room, which is highlighted with bamboo furniture. *Poha*-glazed rack of lamb, Vietnamese spring rolls, pastas, sashimi and hamburgers with salsa are favorites at this Four Seasons restaurant. Deluxe to ultra-deluxe.

Seasons (3900 Wailea Alanui Drive, Wailea; 874-8000), the signature restaurant at the Four Seasons Resort Wailea, gained a vaunted reputation soon after it opened several years ago. Marble trim, chairs upholstered in leather and knockout ocean views create the suitable ambience. But it is the cuisine for which the dining room is particularly known. Specializing in fresh fish and locally grown produce prepared in a blend of American and Mediterranean styles, it is one of Maui's top restaurants. Ultra-deluxe.

The Grand Dining Room Maui (3850 Wailea Alanui Drive; 875-1234) offers panoramic views of the Grand Wailea Resort's cascading pool and the Wailea waterfront. This could be your only chance to dine while surrounded by ceramic pineapples, a 260-pound conch shell and 40-foot Hawaiian murals. The atrium restaurant serves up such delectables as roulade of beef tempura, grilled ahi tuna Niçoise, crispy ginger Chinese duck and *tournedos* of veal. Ultra-deluxe.

Lighter fare is available at the Grand Wailea's **Café Kula** (3850 Wailea Alanui Drive; 875-1234), a terrace dining area that specializes in a "cuisine naturelle" menu designed around fruit and produce freshly picked from the fields of upcountry Maui. It's the place to breakfast on fresh fruit smoothies and apple-banana pancakes with a side of turkey bacon. At lunch the spa entrées include a *harissa* couscous, zucchini tart and a *basmati* rice torta. Moderate.

Chandeliers suspended from vaulted ceilings illuminate **Kea Lani/ The Restaurant** (4100 Wailea Alanui Drive, Wailea; 808-875-4100) at the Kea Lani Hotel. Reminiscent of a grand Greek villa, this dining room offers specialties such as wild mushroom strudel, Dungeness crab cakes, smoked rack of wild boar and mahimahi pan-seared with grilled shrimp. For dessert why not try the local version of Baked Alaska, appropriately renamed "Baked Hawaii"? Ultra-deluxe.

For moderate-to-deluxe-priced fare, consider the *kiawe*-grilled hamburgers or the salads at the Kea Lani's **Polo Beach Grille and Bar** (4100 Wailea Alanui Drive, Wailea; 808-875-4100). This poolside dining spot is also a great place for an umbrella drink.

A tranquil oceanfront setting makes the **Prince Court** (5400 Makena Alanui Drive, Makena; 874-1111) the place to enjoy Hawaiian regional cuisine. At this signature restaurant in the Maui Prince Hotel, you can choose from a menu that begins with shellfish on shaved ice, Maui onion *chèvre* tart and conch chowder. The bill of fare continues with *kiawe*-grilled shrimp in wild lime leaf marinade and filet mignon with foie gras and island shrimp. Spacious booths, wicker furniture and tropical foliage add to the elegance. Entrées at the Prince Court range in price from deluxe to ultra-deluxe.

Hakone (5400 Makena Alanui Drive, Makena; 874-1111) is the kind of restaurant you'd expect to find at any self-respecting Japanese-owned resort. The *shoji* screens, Japanese fans and a sushi bar are authentic; the ocean views are entirely Hawaiian. Start with yakitori or miso soup. Entrées include sashimi, sukiyaki and grilled sirloin steak with *ponzu* sauce. Ultra-deluxe.

KIHEI-WAILEA AREA SHOPPING

Shopping in Kihei is centered in the malls and doesn't hold a lot of promise. You'll find swimwear shops and an assortment of other clothing outlets, but nothing with style and panache. Foremost among the malls is **Azeka Place Shopping Center**, which stretches along the 1200 South block of Kihei Road.

Kukui Mall just down the road has that most wonderful of inventions—a bookstore: a **Waldenbooks** (874-3688) bookstore to be exact.

If you don't find what you're searching for at any of these addresses, there are countless other strip malls along Kihei Road.

Or, if you prefer more sophisticated shops, continue on to Wailea. The elite counterpart to Kihei, this resort complex features two dozen different stores in **Wailea Shopping Village**.

Each year the Kai Lani Hotel hosts a **Marine Art Expo** (4100 Wailea Alanui Drive, Wailea; 875-4100). Held during February and March, the event brings together painters and sculptors from Hawaii, the mainland United States, Australia and other countries. You're likely to find sea turtles depicted on etched-glass vases, 14-karat gold necklaces with dolphins and humpback whales, cibachrome dolphin phones and stoneware wallhangings that re-create brilliantly colored tropical fish.

Jewels Wailea (3700 Wailea Alanui Drive, Wailea; 879-1922) sells pearls and custom accessories made by leading Maui artisans. In the Maui Inter-Continental Resort, this shop is a good place to find original designs in rings, necklaces and pendants.

Much of the $30 million art collection in the Grand Wailea Resort and Spa comes from the personal holdings of the owner, Takeshi Sekiguchi. At the hotel's **Napua Gallery** (3850 Wailea Alanui Drive, Wailea; 875-1234), you can see some of his best Picasso lithographs, including *Les Deux Femmes Nues*. This series focuses on Picasso's longtime companion, Françoise Gilot, and demonstrates the artist's personal evolution. Also available for purchase are paintings, mixed media works and sculpture by leading contemporary Hawaiian artists.

The **Dolphin Gallery** (Wailea Alanui Drive, Wailea; 875-1234) is the place to look for sculpture, art and jewelry with an emphasis on marine mammals. This Grand Hyatt shop has everything from bronzes to earrings.

In an imaginative blend of local and European fashion designs, antique aloha shirts, Balinese sarongs, hippie dresses and Panama hats are just some of the attractions at the Kea Lani Hotel's **Mango Club** (4100 Wailea Alanui Drive, Wailea; 875-4100).

Mandalay Imports (3900 Wailea Alanui Drive, Wailea; 874-5111) is the place to find Thai silk, designer dresses, lacquer chests, Chinese opera coats, beaded belts and Balinese art. This shop in the Four Seasons Resort Wailea also sells innovative necklaces and ceramic vases.

For sportswear and casual evening outfits, try **Collections** (5400 Makena Alanui Drive, Makena; 874-1111) at the Maui Prince Hotel. Bathing suits, aloha shirts and whimsical earrings are all on the menu.

KIHEI-WAILEA AREA NIGHTLIFE

Every Wednesday night, **Luigi's Pasta & Pizzeria** (Azeka Place Shopping Center, 1280 South Kihei Road, Kihei; 879-4446) remakes the third tier of its multideck restaurant into a dancefloor. Despite the deejay spinning platters, the place still looks like a converted restaurant, but it's the hottest spot in Kihei's lukewarm night scene. In addition to dancing, there's karaoke on Friday and Saturday night.

The Maui Lu Resort's **Longhouse** (879-5881) features a Polynesian revue every Wednesday.

The **Sunset Terrace Lounge** (3550 Wailea Alanui Drive, Wailea; 879-4900) is a nifty spot to see live Hawaiian entertainment as day turns to night. It's located at the Stouffer Wailea Beach Resort, where you can also enjoy a quiet drink to the tinkle of a piano at **Raffles**.

Top-40 and big-band tunes waft through the air beneath the tentlike canopy of the Maui Inter-Continental's **Inu Inu Lounge** (3700 Wailea Alanui Drive; 879-1922). This safari-style establishment—adorned with tribal art and faux leopardskin banquettes—is *the* place to dance to live music Tuesday through Saturday.

Live Hawaiian entertainment is a nightly feature at the Maui Inter-Continental Resort's **Hula Terrace** (Wailea Alanui Drive, Wailea; 879-1922). Come for dinner at the Hula Moons or have a drink as you enjoy one of the island's best shows.

Leave it to the Grand Wailea Resort Hotel and Spa (the accent's on Grand) to have Maui's most elaborate high-tech nightclub. **Tsunami** (3850 Wailea Alanui Drive, Wailea; 875-1234) cost $4 million to build and has 20 video monitors and a 14-foot-wide karaoke screen. Cover on the weekend.

A trio plays contemporary classics on the terrace of **Seasons** (3900 Wailea Alanui Drive, Wailea; 874-8000). A second venue here at the Four Seasons Resort Wailea is the **Cabana Café**, where live Hawaiian music and dancing is perfectly timed for a sunset drink.

There is a Hawaiian soloist performing nightly at the **Molokini Lounge** (5400 Makena Alanui Drive; 874-1111) over in Makena at the Maui Prince Hotel.

KIHEI-WAILEA AREA BEACHES AND PARKS

Kihei Beach, a narrow, palm-fringed beach that runs from Maalaea Bay to Kihei, can be seen from several points along Kihei Road and is accessible from the highway. The entire stretch is dotted with small parks and picnic areas and doesn't actually go by a specific name. There are buildings and numerous condominiums along this strip, but few large crowds on the beach. Beach joggers take note: You can run for miles along this unbroken strand, but watch for heavy winds in the afternoon. There are picnic tables and restrooms at Kihei Memorial Park, which is midway along the beach. Shallow weed-ridden waters make for poor swimming and only fair snorkeling (you'll find better at Kamaole beaches). For those anglers in the crowd, bonefish, *papio*, mullet, goatfish, *ulua*, *moano* and mountain bass are all caught here.

Kalama County Beach Park (South Kihei Road, across from Kihei Town Center) is a long, broad park that has an ample lawn but very little beach. Rather than lapping along the sand, waves wash up against a stone seawall. Backdropped by Haleakala, Kalama has stunning views of West Maui, Lanai and Kahoolawe. This is an excellent place for a picnic but, before you pack your lunch, remember that the park, like all Kihei's beaches, is swept by afternoon winds. There are picnic areas, restrooms, showers and tennis courts. For surfers there are summer breaks over a coral reef; left and right slides. Snorkeling and fishing are fair; swimming is poor.

Strung like beads along the Kihei shore are the three beautiful **Kamaole Beach Parks** (I, II and III), their white sands fringed with grass and studded with trees. With Haleakala in the background, they all offer magnificent views of the West Maui Mountains, Lanai and Kahoolawe—and all are windswept in the afternoon. The parks are on South Kihei Road near Kihei Town Center. Each is equipped with picnic areas, restrooms and showers. Kamaole III also has a playground. Swimming is very good on all three beaches. The best snorkeling is near the rocks fringing Kamaole III. Common catches include bonefish, *papio*, mullet, goatfish, *ulua*, *moano* and mountain bass.

Ho hum, yet another beautiful white-sand beach . . . Like other nearby parks, **Keawakapu Beach,** on South Kihei Road between Kihei and Wailea, has marvelous views of the West Maui Mountains and Lanai, but is plagued by afternoon winds. The half-mile-long beach is bordered on both ends by lava points. The swimming is good, but Keawakapu is not as well protected as the Kamaole beaches are. Snorkelers, try the area around the rocks. Surfing, too, is good here and the fishing is excellent. There are no facilities except showers, but it is only a short distance to the markets and restaurants of Kihei and Wailea.

Mokapu and **Ulua** are two crescent-shaped beaches fringed with palms and looking out toward Lanai and Kahoolawe. Much of their natural beauty has been spoiled by the nearby hotel and condominium developments. To get there, follow the signs near Stouffer's Wailea Beach Hotel. The beaches have landscaped miniparks and are popular with bodysurfers. Swimming and snorkeling are both good; restrooms and showers are available.

Wailea Beach, another lovely white-sand strip, once fringed with *kiawe* trees, is now dominated by two very large, very upscale resorts, part of the ultramodern Wailea development here. Swimming is good (the beach is popular with bodysurfers) and so is snorkeling. Restrooms and showers are available. The beach is adjacent to the Four Seasons Wailea Resort just a half-mile south of Wailea Shopping Village.

Though not quite as attractive as Wailea Beach, **Polo Beach** still has a lot to offer. There's a bountiful stretch of white sand and great views of Kahoolawe and Molokini. You'll find it about one mile south of Wailea Shopping Village. The beach has a landscaped minipark, restrooms and showers and is popular with bodysurfers. Swimming is good here and the snorkeling is excellent.

Poolenalena (or **Paipu**) **Beach Park** is a lovely white-sand beach that has been transformed into an attractive little facility frequented by people from throughout the area. Next to Makena, it is the prettiest beach in the Kihei-Wailea region. On Makena Alanui about seven miles south of Wailea Shopping Village, the beach has no facilities, but is only two miles from the market in Wailea. Swimming is good, snorkeling fair and fishing very good—many species are caught here. There is unofficial tent camping here under the *kiawe* trees that front the beach but it is illegal and you can be arrested.

The long, narrow, salt-and-pepper beach located just north of Red Hill, a shoreline cinder cone, is known locally as **Black Sands Beach** or **Oneuli Beach**. Fringed with *kiawe* trees, this stretch of beach is less attractive but more secluded than Makena is. To reach it, follow Makena Alanui south from Wailea Shopping Village for three-and-three-quarters miles. Turn right on the dirt road at the north end of Red Hill, then bear right to the beach. Facilities are nonexistent and it's four miles to the market in Wailea. Swimming and snorkeling are both fair, but the fishing is very good, many species being caught here. There is unofficial camping but, again, it is illegal and not recommended.

MAKENA LANDING

Now a peaceful cove, Makena Landing was once a port as busy as Lahaina. During the California Gold Rush, prevailing winds prompted many San Francisco-bound ships coming up from Cape Horn to resupply here. Fresh fruits and vegetables, badly needed by the would-be miners, were traded in abundance. Later local ranchers delivered their cattle to market by tethering them to longboats and swimming the animals out to steamers waiting just offshore from Makena Landing.

Much more than a beach, **Makena** (or **Oneloa**) **Beach** is an institution. For over a decade, it's been a countercultural gathering place. There are even stories about rock stars jamming here during Makena's heyday in the early 1970s. Once a hideaway for hippies, the beach today is increasingly popular with straight tourists. So far this long, wide corridor of white sand curving south from Red Hill is still the most beautiful beach on Maui, but it is slated for mondo-condo development.

Little Makena Beach (**Puu Olai Beach**), a pretty stretch of white sand next to Makena Beach, just across Red Hill, is a nude beach. It's also popular with the island's gay crowd. But if you go nude here or at Makena, watch out for police; they regularly bust nudists. To get there, follow Makena Alanui for about four-and-one-half miles south from Wailea Shopping Village. Watch for Red Hill, the large cinder cone on your right. Just past Red Hill, turn right onto the paved road and continue to the beach. Swimming is good (bodysurfing is especially good at Little Makena) and you can snorkel near the rocks at the north end of the beach. The fishing is fair. Camping though unofficial is very popular here, but beware of thieves. There are no facilities.

SEVEN

Kahului-Wailuku Area

The island's commercial and civic centers, as well as the greatest concen- **129** tration of Maui residents, are located in the adjoining cities of Kahului and Wailuku. With no clear dividing place, these two municipalities seem at first glance to be "twin towns." They drift into one another as you climb uphill from Kahului Harbor toward the mountains. Kahului is significantly younger than its neighbor, however, and focuses its daily life around commerce. Maui's main airport is here, together with a skein of shopping malls and a few hotels lining a blue-collar waterfront. Wailuku presents a more rolling terrain and is the seat of government for Maui County.

Kahului, with its bustling harbor and busy shopping complexes, offers little to the sightseer. The piers along the waterfront, lined with container-cargo ships and weekly cruise ships, are the embarkation point for Maui's sugar and pineapple crops. Established as a sugar town more than a century ago, Kahului has a commercial feel about it.

Coming from the airport along Kaahumanu Avenue (Route 32), you can wander through **Kanaha Pond Wildlife Sanctuary**. Once a royal fishpond, this is now an important bird refuge, especially for the rare Hawaiian stilt and Hawaiian coot.

The highway leads uphill to **Wailuku**, Maui's administrative center. Older and more interesting than Kahului, Wailuku sits astride the foothills of the West Maui Mountains. A mix of woodframe plantation houses and suburban homes, it even boasts a multi-story civic building. For a short tour of the aging woodfront quarter, take a right on Market Street and follow it several blocks to **Happy Valley**. This former red-light district still retains the charm, if not the action, of a bygone era. Here you'll discover narrow streets and tinroof houses framed by the sharply rising, deeply creased face of the West Maui Mountains.

For a peek at some examples of the wild boars and feral goats that roam Hawaii's wilderness areas, stop at **Maui Zoological and Botanical Gardens** (Kanaloa Avenue, Wailuku; 243-7337). This children's zoo also features a variety of brightly colored tropical birds, as well as ostriches, ducks, geese and monkeys. You can also wander through the botanical garden, which contains an array of native Hawaiian plants.

The county government buildings reside along High Street. Just across the road rests picturesque **Kaahumanu Church** (244-5189). Queen Kaahumanu attended services here in 1832 when the church was a grass shack, and requested that the first permanent church be named after her. Now Maui's oldest church, this grand stone-and-plaster structure was constructed in 1876, and has been kept in excellent condition for its many visitors. With a lofty white spire, it is the area's most dramatic manmade landmark.

Nearby you'll find the **Bailey House Museum** (2375-A Main Street; 244-3326; admission), run by the Maui Historical Society museum. Housed in the home of a former missionary, the displays include 19th-century Hawaiian artifacts, remnants from the early sugarcane industry and period pieces from the missionary years. This stone-and-plaster house (completed in 1850) has walls 20 inches thick and beams fashioned from hand-hewn sandalwood. Together with an adjoining seminary building, it harkens back to Wailuku's days as an early center of western culture.

Bounded on both sides by the sharp walls of Iao Valley, **Tropical Gardens of Maui** (244-3085; admission) encompasses four densely planted acres of fruit trees, orchids and flowering plants. Iao Stream rushes through the property, which offers garden paths and a lily pond.

Just up the road at **Kepaniwai County Park**, there's an outdoor cultural showcase to discover. Backdropped by Iao Valley's adze-like peaks, this adult playground features lovely Japanese and Chinese monuments as well as a taro patch. There are arched bridges, a swimming pool and an Oriental garden. The houses of Hawaii's many cultural groups are represented by a Hawaiian grass hut, New England saltbox (complete with white picket fence), Japanese bamboo house and a Portuguese villa. It was on this site in 1790 that Kamehameha's forces overwhelmed the army of a Maui chief in a battle so terrible that the corpses blocking Iao Stream gave Kepaniwai ("damming of the waters") and Wailuku ("bloody river") their names.

Uphill at the **John F. Kennedy Profile** you'll see Hawaii's answer to Mt. Rushmore, chiseled by nature. Ironically, this geologic formation, which bears an uncanny resemblance to the former president, was never noticed until after his assassination.

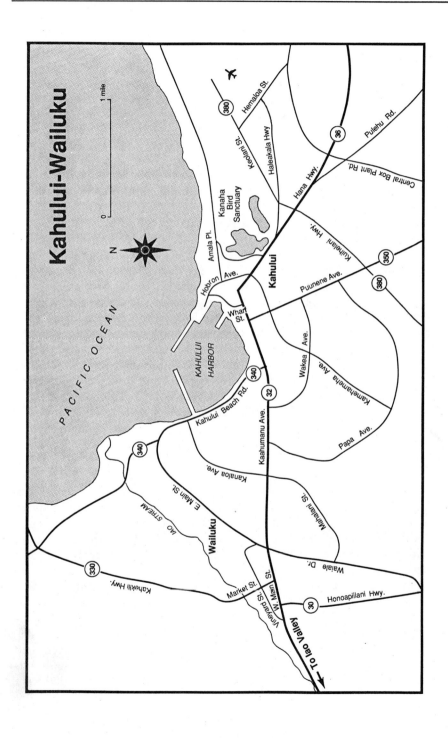

Iao Valley State Monument, surrounded by those same moss-mantled cliffs, provides an excellent view of **Iao Needle**, a single spire that rises to a point 1200 feet above the valley (and 2250 feet above sea level). With the possible exception of Haleakala Crater, this awesome peak is Maui's most famous landmark. A basalt core that has withstood the ravages of erosion, the "Needle" and mist-filled valley have long been a place of pilgrimage for Hawaiians. (Be sure to explore the paths from the parking lot that lead across Iao Stream and up to a vista point.)

KAHULUI-WAILUKU AREA LODGING

The hotel strip in the harbor town of Kahului lies along the beach on Kahului Bay.

The **Maui Seaside Hotel** (100 Kaahumanu Avenue; 877-3311) consists of two separate complexes sitting beside each other along Kaahumanu Avenue (Route 32). There is a pool, restaurant and lounge. Rooms in the older poolside wing are a bit less expensive: Clean, but lacking in decorative flair, the surroundings are quite adequate. Just a few well-spent dollars more places you in a larger, more attractive room in the newer complex, which has more upscale appointments. Both facilities feature telephones, televisions and air conditioning. Some include kitchenettes. Moderate to deluxe.

The nearby **Maui Palms Hotel** (170 Kaahumanu Avenue; 877-0071) has comfortable and spacious rooms at moderate prices with wall-to-wall carpeting, telephone and color television, but lacks decoration. This beachfront facility has a pool tucked between the lobby and the rooms. There's also an Asian-American restaurant on the premises that provides a convenient dining facility for folks staying anywhere along Kahului's hotel row. The grounds are studded with palms; considering the price, the ambience is quite appealing.

Even by Maui's mellow standards, life at the **Banana Bungalow** (310 North Market Street, Wailuku; 244-5090) is *low* key. When I stopped by there was no one around. The rooms—plain, clean units with shared baths—are among the cheapest on the island. There are shared facilities with two to a room as well as private singles and doubles. A cross between a hotel and a hostel, you'll find Banana Bungalow has an ambience unlike any place else on Maui. Community breakfast and dinner are available for a small donation. Television lounge; laundry facilities; budget.

Northshore Inn (2080 Vineyard Street, Wailuku; 242-8999) is another clean, trim hostel-cum-hotel with shared rooms and private singles or doubles at budget rates. The lobby/television room is decorated with surfboards, flags and modern art, and the place has an easy, wind-swept air about it. There are laundry and kitchen facilities; baths are shared. Every room has a refrigerator and overhead fan.

Kahului, then Maui's largest town, was deliberately destroyed by fire in 1890 to kill rats that were spreading an epidemic of bubonic plague.

KAHULUI-WAILUKU AREA RESTAURANTS

The best place in Kahului for a quick, inexpensive meal is at one of several shopping arcades along Kaahumanu Avenue (Route 32). For common fare, head over to the Maui Mall. Here you can drop in at **Restaurant Matsu** (871-0822), a short-order eatery that features such Japanese selections as tempura, yakitori, sushi and *saimin*. Next door at **Siu's Chinese Kitchen** (871-0828), they serve *dim sum* and other Chinese specialties. To round off the calorie count, you can try a cup of *guri guri* sherbet at **Tasaka Guri Guri Shop** (871-4513). All are budget-priced.

For good, inexpensive Chinese food, join the locals at **Ming Yen** (162 Alamaha Street, Kahului; 871-7787). The decor is functional and plain, but the Cantonese and Szechuan selections make up for it. Favorite Szechuan dishes include crispy duck with fragrant sauce, mu shu pork and spicy Szechuan eggplant. On the milder side are Cantonese standbys such as lemon chicken and sweet and sour pork. Budget.

If you're staying at one of Kahului's bayfront hotels, you might try **Vi's Restaurant** (Kaahumanu Avenue; 871-6494) in the Maui Seaside Hotel. This open-air Polynesian-style establishment has seafood and other assorted dinners. The ambience here is quite pleasant, and the staff congenial, but in the past the service has sometimes been slow. Vi doesn't serve lunch, but at breakfast time (7 to 9:30 a.m.) the daily specials might include T-bone steak and eggs or banana hot cakes. Moderate.

The **East-West Dining Room** (877-0071) lies along Kaahumanu Avenue in the Maui Palms Hotel. This spacious open-air restaurant looks past the hotel lawn out over Kahului Bay. True to its name, the East-West serves a Japanese buffet at dinner, and at lunch features American cuisine. Both the lunch and evening buffets are comfortably priced. The latter includes shrimp tempura, scallops, mixed vegetables, yakitori chicken, teriyaki steak, many different types of Japanese salad and a host of other dishes. Moderate.

It's locals only (and that is *never* a bad sign!) at **Wolfgang's Bistro Garden** (Kaahumanu and Lono avenues, Kahului; 871-7555). Accented in hardwood and etched glass, Wolfgang's serves Continental cuisine. The lunch specialty is *spaetzle*; at dinner it's stuffed cornish game hen served in a clay pot that's yours to take home. Though deluxe in price, Wolfgang's has a moderate-priced early-bird menu from 5:00 to 6:30 p.m.

At **The Chart House** (500 North Puunene Avenue, Kahului; 877-2476) you can lean back in a captain's chair and gaze past the woodwork and candlelight out over Kahului Bay. There's a lavish salad-bar-in-the-round centered in the main dining room, an open grill just to the side and a cozy bar off in the wings. The menu offers a surf-and-turf selection with many dishes. Deluxe.

Up the road apiece in Wailuku there are numerous ethnic restaurants guaranteed to please both the palate and the purse. **Sam Sato's** (1750 Wili Pa Loop; 244-7124) features Japanese and American cuisine. Open for breakfast and lunch, it specializes in *manju* (a bean cake pastry), dry *mein* (a noodle dish) and the ubiquitous *saimin*. The nearby **Fujiya** (133 Market Street; 244-0206) stirs up some similar money-belt-tightening Asian meals. Either place is well worth a visit.

Siam Thai Cuisine (123 North Market Street, Wailuku; 244-3817) is always a good choice for Southeast Asian fare. Attractively decorated with posters and artworks from Thailand, this restaurant features a complete menu that includes dozens of delicious dishes. Try the chicken-coconut soup, *tom-yum goong,* Siam chicken, or the *pod-pet,* beef or pork or chicken sautéed with ginger and bamboo shoots. With its budget prices, this is a local favorite.

If it's a cheeseburger you're craving, a *real* cheeseburger, then to the **Vineyard Tavern** (2171 Vineyard Street, Wailuku; 244-9597) you go. There is no table service; you order from the bartender, but ambience is of little consequence when great hamburgers are on the menu. They are half-pound affairs, flame-broiled as you watch, and there's a salad bar and ice-cold beer to make the meal complete. Note: people have been known to come from as far as Japan to enjoy these culinary masterpieces. Budget.

Local, budget-priced and attractively decorated—what more can you ask? Well, **Chums** (1900 Main Street, Wailuku; 244-1000) will go one more and add tasty food. Settle into a hardwood booth and order from an island-style menu that includes saimin, won ton soup, curry stew, teriyaki pork and mahimahi. Or stay middle-of-the-road with a sandwich or salad.

Saeng's Thai Cuisine (2119 Vineyard Street, Wailuku; 244-1567) sits in a beautifully designed building embellished with fine woodwork and adorned with Asian accoutrements. The menu, which lists six pages of dishes from Thailand, is like an encyclopedia of fine dining. Meals, served in the dining room or out on a windswept veranda, begin with *sateh* and spring rolls, venture on to dishes like the "evil prince" and "tofu delight," and end over tea and tapioca pudding. Budget to moderate.

Wailuku is becoming more hip by the month, and the center of "hip-dom" is an espresso house with a hand-painted floor, upstairs dining room with ocean views and a pizza/quesadilla/salad menu. At **Café Kup a Kuppa** (79 Church Street; 244-0500) you can order scrambled eggs or bagel with lox and cream cheese for breakfast; lunch includes chicken, turkey, vegetable or tuna sandwiches, and daily specials like quiche; no dinner; budget.

Like its Waikiki counterpart, **Hamburger Mary's** (2010 Main Street, Wailuku; 244-7776) is a center for gays. Imaginatively decorated with surfboards and antique posters, it attracts a mixed clientele with an appealing menu of hamburgers (who would have guessed?), sandwiches, salads and steaks. There's also a hearty breakfast menu. Moderate.

Wailuku's low-rent district lies along Lower Main Street, where a string of ethnic restaurants caters almost exclusively to local residents. These are informal, family-owned, formica-and-naugahyde-chair cafés that serve good food at budget prices. You'll find Japanese food at **Tokyo Tei** (1063 Lower Main Street; 242-9630), while Southeast Asia is represented by **A Touch of Saigon** (1246 Lower Main Street; 244-7845).

KAHULUI-WAILUKU AREA SHOPPING

For everyday shopping needs, you should find the Kahului malls very convenient. Three sprawling centers are strung along Kaahumanu Avenue (Route 32).

Kaahumanu Center is the best and most modern, with **Liberty House** (877-3361) and **Sears** (877-2221), a photo studio, **Waldenbooks** (871-6112), boutiques, shoe stores, candy stores, a sundries shop and a jeweler. For Japanese gourmet foods, try **Cherokee** (877-5551) in the Kaahumanu Center.

Nearby **Maui Mall** has a similar inventory of shops. **Sir Wilfred's Tobacconist** (877-3711) stocks a connoisseur's selection of tobaccos and coffees, and even has a coffee bar.

You might also try **Kahului Shopping Center**, though I prefer the other, more convenient malls.

Up in Wailuku, a tumbledown town with a friendly face, you'll find the little shops and solicitous merchants that we have come to associate with small-town America. Along North Market Street you'll discover several imaginative shops operated by low-key entrepreneurs. There's **Traders of the Lost Ark** (62 North Market Street; 242-7753), with ancestral carvings and art from Africa, Asia and the Pacific, as well as

---

MADE ON MAUI

*En route to the airport with limited time to shop for souvenirs? Not to worry. Simply stop off at **Maui Tropical Plantation** (Route 30, Waikapu; 244-7643), where the Made-on-Maui marketplace stocks macadamia nut caramel corn, Maui potato chips and fudge bento boxes. Or, if it's a nosegay you're sniffing out, you can pick up heliconia and plumeria at the plantation's tropical nursery.*

Aloha shirts, Oriental rugs, jewelry and temple rubbings; **Memory Lane** (158 North Market Street; 244-4196), featuring antiques and unusual collectibles; and **Wailuku Gallery** (28 North Market Street; 244-4544), which specializes in works by Maui artists.

Some of the island's most reasonably priced souvenirs are found at the **Maui Historical Society Museum Gift Shop** (2375-A Main Street, Wailuku; 244-3326). Here you'll find an outstanding collection of local history books and art prints. Quilts and *koa* bookmarks are also popular.

There are rasta posters and T-shirts, plus a colorful inventory of island wear, at **Maui Reggae Connection** (10 North Market Street, Wailuku; 242-8858).

A Touch of Glass (1977 Main Street, Wailuku; 871-6694) has an array of original and amazingly beautiful stained-glass pieces. This studio/gallery even offers courses in the art.

KAHULUI-WAILUKU AREA NIGHTLIFE

If Kahului can be said to have an entertainment strip, Kaahumanu Avenue (Route 32) is the place. You can enjoy a live band and dancing at the **Maui Palms Hotel** (877-0071) on Saturday nights. The nearby **Red Dragon Room**, at the Maui Beach Hotel (877-0051), also fires up every Saturday night by rolling back the banquet tables and wheeling in the Red Dragon Disco. There's a cover and two-drink minimum.

Up in Wailuku, **Aki's** (309 North Market Street; 244-8122) entertains a local crowd almost every night around its bar. Located in Wailuku's Happy Valley section, it's a good place to meet people, or just to sit back and enjoy a tall, cool drink.

Another neighborhood hangout just up the street and around the corner is the **Vineyard Tavern** (2171 Vineyard Boulevard; 244-9597). With a falsefront exterior and swinging doors, this establishment is reminiscent of a Wild West saloon. The jukebox music is cowboy contemporary yet the ambience is definitely Mauian.

MAUI'S FAMOUS POTATO CHIPS

Always a favorite with locals, Maui's potato chips have now become a worldwide phenomenon. One of the most popular brands is "Kitch'n Cook'd," made at the family-owned and operated Maui Potato Chip Factory (295 Lalo Place, off Highway 36, Kahului; 877-3652). This place has been around since the 1950s, annually increasing in popularity, and it now brings in orders from around the globe. These chips are hard to find in mainland stores, but you can stock up on them here where they're freshly made!

The gay nightspot on Maui is **Hamburger Mary's** (2010 Main Street, Wailuku; 244-7776), an attractive watering hole with overhead fans and a collection of antique wallhangings worthy of a museum. There's deejay music and dancing nightly. Attracting both gay men and women, Hamburger Mary's also draws a straight crowd, especially on Tuesday and Thursday nights when the cruise ship is in port.

KAHULUI-WAILUKU AREA BEACHES AND PARKS

Hoaloha Park (Kaahumanu Avenue, Route 32), next to the Kahului hotels, is Kahului's only beach, but unfortunately the nearby harbor facilities detract from the natural beauty of its white sands. What with heavy boat traffic on one side and several hotels on the other, the place is not recommended. Swimming and snorkeling are poor; surfers will find good breaks (two to six feet, with a left slide) off the jetty mouth near the north shore of Kahului Harbor. It is, however, a good spot, to beachcomb, particularly for Maui diamonds. Picnic tables are available. Goatfish, *papio* and triggerfish can be hooked from the pier; *ulua* and *papio* are often caught along the shore.

The beautiful **Kepaniwai County Park**, in Wailuku on the road to Iao Valley, is surrounded by sheer cliffs. You'll discover paths over arched bridges and through gardens, plus pagodas, a thatch-roofed hut, a taro patch and banana, papaya and coconut trees. An ideal and romantic spot for picnicking, it has picnic pavilions, restrooms and a swimming pool.

Waihee Beach Park, outside Wailuku on the rural road that circles the West Maui Mountains is used almost exclusively by local residents. Bordered by a golf course and shaded with ironwood trees and *naupaka* bushes, it has a sandy beach and one of Maui's longest and widest reefs. There's a grassy area perfect for picnicking, established picnic areas and restrooms with showers. Beachcombing, *limu* gathering, fishing, swimming and snorkeling are all good. To get there from Route 340 in Waiehu, turn right on Halewaiu Road and then take the beach access road from Waiehu Golf Course.

Central Maui

Central Maui is defined not by what it is but by what lies to the east and west of it. On one side Haleakala lifts into the clouds; on the other hand loom the West Maui mountains, a folded landscape over 5000 feet in elevation. Between them, at the center of the island, sits an isthmus planted in sugar cane and pineapple. Never rising more than a few hundred feet above sea level, it houses Kahului along its northern edge and serves as the gateway to both the Lahaina–Kaanapali and Kihei–Wailea areas.

Three highways cross the isthmus separating West Maui from the slopes of Haleakala. From Kahului, Mokulele Highway (Route 350) tracks south to Kihei through this rich agricultural area. The Kuihelani Highway (Route 380), running diagonally across sugarcane plantations, joins the Honoapiilani Highway (Route 30) in its course from Wailuku along the West Maui Mountains. The low-lying area that supports this network of roadways was formed by lava flows from Haleakala and the West Maui Mountains.

The **Alexander & Baldwin Sugar Museum** (Puunene Avenue and Hansen Road, Puunene; 871-8058; admission), situated on the grounds of a working plantation, provides a brief introduction to Hawaii's main crop. Tracing the history of sugar cultivation in the islands, its displays portray everything from early life in the cane fields to contemporary methods for producing refined sugar.

Along Honoapiilani Highway (Route 30), the road to Lahaina, lies **Maui Tropical Plantation** (244-7643; admission for the tram), a 120-acre enclave complete with orchards and groves displaying dozens of island fruit plants. Here you'll see avocados, papayas, bananas, pineapples, mangoes and macadamia nuts growing in lush profusion. There's a tropical nursery, museum, aquaculture display and a tram that will carry you through this ersatz plantation. Ask about the plantation's dinner/tour/show special. On Monday, Tuesday and Thursday evenings you can enjoy a guided tour, cocktails, cookout dinner and a Hawaiian-style musical revue for one all-inclusive price.

MOLOKINI

Molokini, a crescent-shaped crater off Maui's southern coast, offers one of the island's great snorkeling adventures. Every day dozens of boatloads of people pull up to dive the remarkably clear waters. Visibility typically ranges between 80 and 150 feet, conditions so clear you can spot fish before even entering the water. During winter months, you're also likely to see the humpback whales cavorting nearby. The 46-foot **Kai Kanani** *(879-7218), which departs from Makena Beach, is the touring vessel closest to this largely submerged volcano. Other companies operating excursions include* **Lahaina Divers** *(710 Front Street, Lahaina; 667-7496),* **Hawaiian Reef Divers** *(129 Lahainaluna Road, Lahaina; 667-7647) and* **Greenpeace Hawaii** *(101 North Kihei Road, Kihei; 879-8188). You can also sail to the islet on the* **Silent Lady** *(Maalaea Harbor; 242-6499), a 64-foot whaling schooner. Most tours include snorkeling equipment, food and drinks in the price of admission*

The first sugar plantation laborers on Maui began to arrive from China in 1852.

Then, as you pass the small boat harbor at **Maalaea Bay**, the highway hugs the southwest coast. There are excellent lookouts along this elevated roadway, especially near the lighthouse at **McGregor Point**. During whale season you might spy a leviathan from this landlocked crow's nest. Just offshore there are prime whale breeding areas.

Down the road from McGregor Point, you'll see three islands anchored offshore. As you look seaward, the portside islet is **Molokini**, the crescent-shaped remains of a volcanic crater.

Kahoolawe, a desiccated island used for naval target practice, sits in the center. Located seven miles off Maui's south coast, it is a bald, windblasted place, hot, arid and home to feral goats. Hawaiian activists are demanding an end to the bombing of this sacred isle and have staged dramatic demonstrations by occupying its forbidden shores.

The humpbacked island to starboard is **Lanai**. Lying eight miles across the Kealaikahiki Channel, it is a pear-shaped island boasting a 3370-foot peak and a population of about 2000 people.

As you continue toward Kaanapali, **Molokai** sails into view. Known as the "Friendly Isle," it covers 260 square miles and contains the highest per capita concentration of native Hawaiians of any of the main islands. With a population of 6700 people, it's a sleepy destination ideal for a Maui getaway excursion.

The road drops back to sea level as it approaches the timeworn village of **Olowalu**. Here, in 1790, more than 100 Hawaiians were slaughtered by the crew of an American ship to avenge the death of a single sailor. Known as the "Olowalu Massacre," this incident contributed significantly to the ill will that developed between the islanders and the interlopers during the next century.

EIGHT

Hana Highway

The Hana Highway (Route 360), a bumpy, tortuous road running be- **141**
tween Kahului and Hana, is one of the most beautiful drives in all Hawaii. Following the path of an ancient Hawaiian trail, it may in fact be
one of the prettiest drives in the world. The road courses through a
rainforest, a luxurious jungle crowded with ferns and African tulip trees,
and leads to black sand beaches and rain-drenched hamlets. The vegetation is so thick it seems to be spilling out from the mountainside in a
cascade of greenery. You'll be traveling the windward side of Haleakala,
hugging its lower slopes en route to a small Hawaiian town that receives
70 inches of rain a year.

There are over 600 twists and turns and 56 one-lane bridges along this
adequately maintained paved road. It will take at least three hours to
drive the 51 miles to Hana. To make the entire circuit around the south
coast, plan either to sleep in Hana or to leave very early and drive all day.
If you can, take your time—there's a lot to see.

About seven miles east of Kahului, you'll pass the quaint, weather-
beaten town of **Paia**. This old sugar plantation town, now a burgeoning
artist colony, has been painted in nursery colors. Along either of Paia's
two streets, falsefront buildings have been freshly refurbished.

On the eastern side of town is the **Mantokuji Buddhist Temple**,
which celebrates the sunrise and sunset every day by sounding its huge
gong 18 times.

Hookipa Beach Park, one of the world's premier windsurfing spots,
lies about three miles east of town. Brilliantly colored sails race along the
horizon as windsurfers perform amazing acrobatic stunts, cartwheeling
across the waves.

Within the next ten miles the roadway is transformed, as your slow, winding adventure begins. You'll drive past sugarcane fields, across verdant gorges, through valleys dotted with tumbledown cottages and along fern-cloaked hillsides.

Route 36 becomes Route 360, beginning a new series of mileage markers that are helpful in locating sites along the way. Near the two-mile marker, a short trail leads to an idyllic swimming hole at **Twin Falls** (the path begins from the west side of the Hoolawa Stream bridge on the right side of the road).

Nearby Huelo, a tiny "rooster town" (so named because nothing ever seems to be stirring except the roosters), is known for the **Kaulanapueo Church**. A coral chapel built in 1853, this New England-style sanctuary strikes a dramatic pose with the sea as a backdrop.

Farther along, on **Waikamoi Ridge**, you'll see picnic areas and a nature trail. Here you can visit a bamboo forest, learn about native vegetation and explore the countryside.

Another picnic area, at **Puohokamoa Falls** (11-mile marker), nestles beside a waterfall and large pool. If you packed a lunch, this is a perfect place to enjoy it. Trails above and below the main pool lead to other waterfalls.

A few zigzags farther, at **Kaumahina State Wayside** (12-mile marker), a tree-studded park overlooks Honomanu Gulch and Keanae Peninsula. From here the road descends the gulch, where a side road leads left to **Honomanu Bay** (14-mile marker) and its black sand beach.

Above Keanae Peninsula, you'll pass the **Keanae Arboretum** (16-mile marker). You can stroll freely through these splendid tropical gardens, which feature many native Hawaiian plants including several dozen varieties of taro. Another section of the gardens is devoted to exotic tropical plants and there is a mile-long trail that leads into a natural rainforest.

Just past the arboretum, turn left onto the road to the **Keanae Peninsula** (17-mile marker). This rocky, windswept point offers stunning views of Haleakala. You'll pass rustic houses, a patchwork of garden plots and a coral-and-stone church built around 1860. A picture of serenity and rural perfection, Keanae is inhabited by native Hawaiians who still grow taro and pound poi. Their home is a lush rainforest—a quiltwork of taro plots, banana trees, palms—that runs to the rim of a ragged coastline.

Another side road descends to **Wailua** (18-mile marker), a Hawaiian agricultural and fishing village. Here is another luxurious checkerboard where taro gardens alternate with banana patches and the landscape is adorned with clapboard houses. The town is known for **St. Gabriel's Church**, a simple structure made completely of sand and coral, dating from 1870.

Back on the main road, there's yet another picnic area and waterfall at **Puaakaa State Wayside** (22-mile marker). The cascade tumbles into a natural pool in a setting framed by eucalyptus and banana trees.

Past here, another side road bumps three miles through picturesque **Nahiku** (25-mile marker) to a bluff overlooking the sea. The view spreads across three bays all the way back to Wailua. Directly below, the ocean pounds against rock outcroppings, spraying salt mist across a stunning

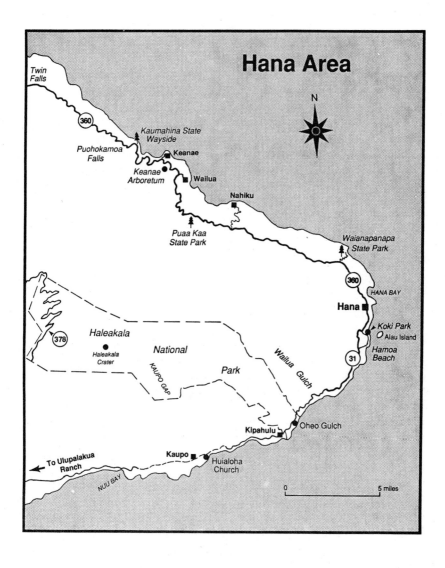

Hana Area

America's first domestic rubber plantation opened in Nahiku in 1905. One can still see a few remaining rubber plants in the area.

vista. Set in one of the wettest spots along the entire coast, Nahiku village is inundated by rainforest and graced by yet another 19th-century church.

For a close-up of the exquisite plant life you've been passing on the Hana Highway, pull off at **Alii Gardens** (Hana Highway, 27-mile marker; 248-7217). This 55-acre flower reserve was planted by Alii Chang, a master gardener. While wandering the trails here, you may feel as if you're seeing flowers from another planet. That's not surprising if you consider that of the 1000 flower species in Hawaii, 90 percent will be found nowhere else in the world.

Several miles before Hana, be sure to stop at **Waianapanapa State Park**. Here you'll find a black sand beach here and two lava tubes, **Waianapanapa** and **Waiomao caves**. Strong swimmers and scuba divers can dive into a pool and swim underwater to reach Waianapanapa Cave, a legendary meeting place for lovers. Hawaiian mythology tells of a Hawaiian princess who hid from her cruel husband here, only to be discovered by him and slain. Now every spring the waters hereabouts are said to run red with her blood. Offshore you will also see several sea arches and nearby a blowhole that spouts periodically.

To reach the secluded hamlet of **Hana**, you can take the old Hawaiian shoreline trail (see the "Hiking" section in Chapter Two) or continue on along the highway. This Eden-like town, carpeted with pandanus, taro and banana trees, sits above an inviting bay. Known as "heavenly Hana," it's a ranch town inhabited primarily by part-Hawaiians. Because of its remote location it has changed little over the years. The rain that continually buffets Hana makes it a prime agricultural area and adds to the luxuriant, unsettling beauty of the place.

Because of its strategic location directly across from the Big Island, Hana was an early battleground in the wars between the chiefs of Maui and the Big Island, who conquered, lost and regained the region in a succession of bloody struggles. During the 19th century it became a sugar plantation, employing different ethnic groups who were brought in to work the fields. Then, in 1946, Paul Fagan, a San Francisco industrialist, bought 14,000 acres and created the Hana Ranch, turning the area into grazing land for Hereford cattle and opening the exclusive Hotel Hana Maui.

Head down to **Hana Bay**. Here you can stroll the beach, explore the wharf and take a short path along the water to a plaque that marks the **Birthplace of Kaahumanu**, King Kamehameha I's favorite wife and a key player in the 1819 overthrow of the ancestral Hawaiian religious system. To reach this sacred spot, pick up the trail leading from the boat landing on the right side of the bay. It leads along the base of **Kauiki Hill**, a cinder cone covered with ironwood trees that was the scene of fierce battles between Kahekili, the renowned Maui chief, and the Big Island chief Kalaniopuu.

Right before the town of Hana, on the right, is **Helani Gardens** (248-8274), a sprawling oasis of tropical plant life. Only a section of the gardens are currently open to the public, but it's worth a stop as they contain a wealth of flowering plants, trees and vines. You'll also find fruit trees, baobab trees, papyrus, ginger plants and even a carp pond. Call ahead to tell them you're coming.

Near the Hotel Hana Maui (where you can request a key to open the gate), you can drive or hike up a short road to **Mount Lyons** (that camel-humped hill with the cross on top). From this aerie, a memorial to Paul Fagan, there's a fine view of Hana Bay and the surrounding coastline.

Also be sure to take in the **Hana Cultural Center** (248-8622). This enticing little gallery displays such artifacts from Hana's past as primitive stone tools, rare shells and Hawaiian games. There are antique photographs and elaborately stitched quilts. Also on the grounds, the old **Court House**, built in 1871, is a modest but appealing structure containing three small benches and a desk for the judge.

Wananalua Church (Hauoli Street and Hana Highway), a lovely chapel built from coral blocks during the mid-19th century, has been beautifully refurbished. Today, services are conducted in English and Hawaiian. Located atop an ancient *heiau*, stately and imposing in appearance, it is a perfect expression of the days when Christianity was crushing the old Hawaiian beliefs.

FROM HANA TO ULUPALAKUA   The backroad from Hana around the southwest side of Maui is one of the island's great adventures. It leads along the side of Haleakala past dense rainforest and tumbling waterfalls to an arid expanse covered by lava flows, and then opens onto Maui's

---

NOTHING IS SACRED

Every tourist to Maui dreams of visiting the "Seven Sacred Pools" at Oheo Gulch in Hana. In fact, says Mark Tanaka-Sanders, a ranger who helps manage a coastal section of Haleakala National Park, "there are 24 pools in the area." Who's responsible for the miscount? "Blame it on the tourist industry," he says. "It's also important to know that the Hawaiian people do not consider these pools sacred."

First opened in 1946, Maui's first resort, the Hotel Hana Maui is still a favorite with both locals and island visitors.

vaunted Upcountry region. Since a five-mile stretch is unpaved and other sections are punctuated with potholes, car rental companies generally do not permit driving on parts of this route; so check with them in advance or be prepared to take your chances. Also check on road conditions: The road is sometimes closed during periods of heavy rain.

Past Hana, the road, now designated the Piilani Highway and renumbered as Route 31 (with mileage markers that descend in sequence), worsens as it winds toward an overgrown ravine where **Wailua Falls** (45-mile marker) and another waterfall pour down sharp cliff faces.

At **Oheo Gulch** (42-mile marker), better known as **Seven Sacred Pools**, a series of waterfalls tumbles into two dozen (not seven!) pools before reaching the sea. The pools are rock-bound, some are bordered by cliffs, and several provide excellent swimming holes. This is an eerie and beautiful place from which you can see up and down the rugged coastline. Used centuries ago by early Hawaiians, they still offer a cool, refreshing experience.

Another special spot, **Charles Lindbergh's grave** (41-mile marker), rests on a promontory overlooking the ocean. The great aviator spent his last days here and lies buried beside Palapala Hoomau Church. The whitewashed chapel and surrounding shade trees create a place of serenity and remarkable beauty. (To find the grave, continue 1.2 miles past Oheo Gulch. Watch for the church through the trees on the left. Turn left onto an unpaved road and drive several hundred yards, paralleling a stone fence. Turn left into the churchyard.)

Not far from here, in **Kipahulu**, the paved road gives way to dirt. It's five miles to the nearest pavement, so your car should have good shock absorbers; sometimes the weather makes it impassable. The road rises along seaside cliffs, some of which are so steep they jut out to overhang the road. This is wild, uninhabited country, ripe for exploration.

Huialoha Church, built in 1859, rests below the road on a wind-wracked peninsula. The last time I visited this aging worship hall, horses were grazing in the churchyard. Nearby you'll encounter the tinroof town of **Kaupo**, with its funky general store. Located directly above the town is **Kaupo Gap**, through which billowing clouds pour into Haleakala Crater.

The road bumps inland, then returns seaward to **Nuu Bay's** rocky beach. From here the rustic route climbs into a desolate area scarred by lava and inhabited with scrub vegetation. The sea views are magnificent as the road bisects the **1790 lava flow**. This was the last volcanic eruption on Maui; it left its mark in a torn and terrible landscape that slopes for miles to the sea.

It's several miles farther until you reach **Ulupalakua Ranch**, a lush counterpoint to the lava wasteland behind. With its grassy acres and curving rangeland, the ranch provides a perfect introduction to Maui's Upcountry region.

HANA HIGHWAY LODGING

Along the Hana Highway out in Paia, about seven miles from Kahului, sits **Nalu Kai Lodge** (579-8009). Tucked behind the Kihata Restaurant near the town hub, this eight-unit resting place is a real sleeper. The last time I was by, only three rooms were available; the others were accommodating permanent residents. If you snag one of the vacant rooms, you'll check into a small, plain cubicle with no carpeting and little decoration. Sound unappealing? Well, even bare walls sometimes look good at low-budget prices.

A very convenient budget-priced accommodation located on the Hana Highway is the **Maui YMCA** (242-9007) in Keanae. For just $8 a night, both men and women are welcome to roll out their sleeping bags on bunks in the dormitory. Set in a spacious wooden house overlooking the sea, this crash pad comes with hot showers. Sorry, the maximum stay here is five nights.

Aloha Cottages (248-8420), perched on a hillside above Hana Bay, has two-bedroom units at moderate prices. Situated amid papaya and banana trees, these cozy cottages feature hardwood floors and walls fashioned from redwood. The decor is simple, the kitchens are all-electric and many of the furnishings are rattan. Representing one of Hana's best

---

HOTEL HANA MAUI

One of Hawaii's finest resting places is the ultra-deluxe-priced Hotel Hana Maui (248-8211), a luxurious retreat on a hillside above the bay. From ocean views to tropical landscape to rolling lawn, this friendly inn is a unique, world-class resort. Spread across the 66-acre grounds are 96 cottages, all elegantly designed and devoid of clocks, radios and televisions. Rates for this getaway of getaways are stratospheric. The hotel's health and fitness complex sponsors a variety of hiking excursions and nature walks. The adjacent 25-meter pool, landscaped with lava walls and monkeypod trees, enjoys a spectacular setting. The staff has been here for generations, lending a sense of home to an enchanting locale. I highly recommended the Hotel Hana Maui.

bargains, the cottages have been recommended many times over the years by readers and friends. There are only five units at this small complex, so advance reservations are a good idea.

You can also consider heading down toward the water to the **Hana Kai Maui Resort** (248-8426). Located smack on a rocky beach, these two twin-story buildings sit amid lush surroundings. The ornamental pool is a freshwater affair fed by toe-dipping spring water. The location and exotic grounds rate a big plus. The bill? A studio apartment or a one-bedroom condominium will price in the deluxe category.

Speaking of scenery, **Heavenly Hana Inn** (248-8442) is blessed indeed. Located about two miles outside Hana, this hostelry offers four suites and is entered through a Japanese gate. On either side, stone lions guard a luxuriant garden. The interior mirrors this elegance. Each two-bedroom apartment is decorated with Japanese screens, bamboo towel racks and Asian art objects. The walls are wood-paneled and the lanai's screened. Ultra-deluxe.

Hana Plantation Houses (248-7248) has everything from homes to cottages to studios. Scattered throughout the Hana area, there are homes with either mountain or ocean views; each unit is fully equipped with kitchens and hot tubs. The wood-paneled accommodations, decorated with tapa-cloth designs and Hawaiian paintings, include a wraparound lanai and interior garden. Most are cooled with Casablanca-style fans and some have outdoor grills perfect for a private luau. Environmentalists will want to check out the solar-powered Waikaloa Beach House. Some facilities are within walking distance of the beach and ancient Hawaiian fishponds. Moderate to ultra-deluxe.

Hana Alii Holidays (248-7742) offers a similar selection of accommodations, ranging from moderately priced studios to homes tabbed in the ultra-deluxe range. Here you can settle into a place on Hana Bay or on an idyllic hillside. Some units sit atop lava-rock bluffs overlooking the ocean, others are found in secluded five-acre settings. All accommodations have full kitchens and most come with lanais and outdoor barbe-

---

SPRING TRAINING, HANA STYLE

In 1946, Hana hosted the only mainland American baseball team ever to conduct spring training in Hawaii. That was the year that financier Paul Fagan brought the Pacific Coast League's San Francisco Seals to the islands. Arriving with the players was a squadron of sportswriters who sent back glowing dispatches on "Heavenly Hana," helping to promote the destination and the Hotel Hana Maui (owned, of course, by Paul Fagan).

cues. Picture windows, *koa*-wood detailing, ceiling fans and decks add to the ambiance.

And don't forget the cabins at **Waianapanapa State Park** (for information, refer to the "Hana Highway Beaches and Parks" section later in this chapter).

HANA HIGHWAY RESTAURANTS

Paia, an artsy little town located just a few miles out on the Hana Highway, has several restaurants to choose from. If you don't choose any of them, however, be forewarned—there are no pit stops between here and Hana.

Wunderbar (89 Hana Highway, Paia; 579-8808) is an uneasy cross between a European dining room and an American bar and grill. You can order a beer at the bar or select from a German menu that includes wienerschnitzel, beef stroganoff and Bavarian hunter steak. They also have full, American-style breakfast and lunch menus. Prices range from moderate to deluxe.

If you're craving a tasty fish sandwich, the **Paia Fish Market** (on the corner of Baldwin Avenue and Hana Highway; 579-8030) is the place to go. If you're not in the mood for seafood, this eatery also offers burgers, pasta and Mexican dishes such as fajitas. With plenty of greenery, and prints of water sports on the walls, this a casual place for a budget-to-moderate-priced meal.

For box lunches, drop in at **Picnics** (30 Baldwin Avenue, Paia; 579-8021). Open for both lunch and dinner, this light and airy café serves a variety of items including spinach-nut burger and mahimahi sandwiches. The menu also offers patrons deli sandwiches and plain old hamburgers at budget prices.

The Vegan Restaurant (115 Baldwin Avenue, Paia; 579-9144) is the prime address hereabouts for vegetarian food. Place your order at the counter—there are salads, sandwiches and hot entrées that include Thai specialties. Budget.

Just down the street you'll find **Kihata Restaurant** (115 Hana Highway, Paia; 579-9035). This old-style restaurant, with bamboo partitions and a screen door that slams, is another favorite watering place for Paia residents. There's a glistening formica counter up front, and a cluster of tables in back. Dining in this local hangout is definitely casual. And the menu is ethnic: In addition to sushi bar specialties, it includes Japanese noodle dishes, *tonkatsu* (deep-fried pork), teriyaki and tempura. But the meals are comfortably priced and the local color is free.

Or, for masterfully prepared food without the sophisticated trappings, try **Mama's Fish House** (on Hana Highway; 579-8488) outside Paia. Unlike most well-heeled restaurants, this oceanfront nook is simply decorated: shell leis, an old Hawaiian photo here, a painting there, plus potted plants. Elegant simplicity. During lunch, there is a varied menu that includes California cuisine-style dishes and ever-changing specialties. Other than a few steak and poultry dishes, the dinner menu is entirely seafood. The evening entrées include abalone, bouillabaisse, scampi and fresh Hawaiian lobster. Another of Mama's treats is fresh fish: There are always at least four varieties, prepared ten different ways. Deluxe to ultra-deluxe.

If you plan to stay in Hana for any length of time, pack some groceries in with the raingear. You'll find only four restaurants along the entire eastern stretch of the island. Luckily, they cover the gamut from budget to ultra-deluxe. **Tutu's At Hana Bay** (248-8224), located within whistling distance of the water, whips up sandwiches, hamburgers and teriyaki chicken for breakfast and lunch. Budget.

Open for breakfast and lunch, **Hana Gardenland Café** (Hana Highway at Kalo Road; 248-8975) offers patio dining overlooking a tropical nursery. The menu includes quiche, pastas, salads and the restaurant has Hana's only complete espresso bar. If you're headed out on a hike, stop here to pick up a picnic lunch.

Hana Ranch Restaurant (248-8255) is a small, spiffy establishment decorated with blond wood and offering great ocean views. There's a full bar here plus a flagstone lanai for outdoor dining. Open daily for lunch, they serve dinner every Friday and Saturday. Lunch is buffet style; in the evening they offer fresh fish, chops, steak and baby back ribs; deluxe. There's also a budget-priced **take-out stand** serving breakfast and lunch, with picnic tables overlooking the ocean.

Hana's premier restaurant is the dining room of the **Hotel Hana Maui** (248-8211). This extraordinary resort, perched on a hillside overlooking the ocean, serves gourmet meals to its guests and the public alike. For lunch the bill of fare includes flank steak with Maui onions, broiled teriyaki chicken breast and sashimi. The evening menu features pan-seared veal chops, steamed Hawaiian snapper and roasted rack of lamb. The menu changes seasonally. Ultra-deluxe.

HANA HIGHWAY SHOPPING

Paia, a rustic falsefront town seven miles outside Kahului, is my favorite place to shop on Maui. Many fine artisans live in the Upcountry area and come down to sell their wares at the small shops lining the Hana Highway. The town itself is a work of art, with old wooden buildings that provide a welcome respite from the crowded shores of Kaanapali and Kihei. I'll mention just the shops I like most. Browse through town to see for yourself. If you discover places I missed, please let me know.

Even celebrities find peace of mind in heavenly Hana. You can join Carol Burnett or George Harrison at the local store.

On display at the **Maui Crafts Guild** (43 Hana Highway; 579-9697) is a range of handmade items all by local artists. Here you'll find anything from pressed hibiscus flowers to bamboo furniture. There are also fabrics, ceramics, jewelry, baskets and other Maui-made items.

Paia Trading Company (106 Hana Highway; 579-9472) has a few interesting antiques and a lot of junk. Among the more noteworthy items: turquoise and silver jewelry, wooden washboards, apothecary jars and antique glassware.

Eddie Flotte Watercolors (83 Hana Highway, Paia; 579-9641) features original artworks by an original character. Flotte's paintings capture the down-home lifestyles of Upcountry residents.

Summerhouse Boutique (83 Hana Highway, Paia; 579-9201) might be called a chic sundries shop. They sell everything from jewelry and postcards to porcelain dolls and natural fiber garments.

Around the corner on Baldwin Avenue lies another shop worth browsing. **The Clothes Addict** (12 Baldwin Avenue; 579-9266) features a fine selection of women's fashions, including designer clothing, manufactured designs and locally made styles. They also have '30s and '40s aloha shirts for men, as well as informal beachwear.

In Hana there are several elegant shops at the Hotel Hana Maui. One of my favorites is **Hana Coast Gallery** (248-8636), which features fine paintings by Maui artists, as well as pieces by the novelist, Henry Miller. Also here are beautiful serigraphs, model racing canoes in *koa*, ceremonial objects, feathered leis, fiber collages and painted tapa cloth.

Exotic tropical flowers make marvelous presents and souvenirs. Visit the 55-acre **Alii Gardens** (27-mile marker; 248-7217) and you'll find colorful heliconia, red and pink ginger plants, orchids, sprouting coconuts and bonsai plants.

For everything you could possibly want or need, drop by the **Hasegawa General Store** (5165 Hana Highway; 248-8231). This store stocks everything from groceries, clothing and hardware to placemats, movie rentals, film and gas. The original Hasegawa's burned down several years ago, but the name is still famous.

Hana Gardenland (Hana Highway at Kalo Road; 248-8975) is a five-acre landscape nursery that seconds as an art gallery. All the orchids, bromeliads and cut flowers can be shipped home. Or you can shop in the gallery for beadwork, *koa* sculpture, tapa cloth and island paintings by Hawaiian artists, including a number from the Hana area.

The **Hana Ranch Trading Company** (248-8211), located at the Hotel Hana Maui, is a good place to shop for Hawaiian shirts, hand-painted bags and *raku* vases.

Also on the grounds of Hotel Hana Maui is **Susan Marie** (248-8211), a shop specializing in sportswear, embroidered shirts and accessories with a tropical flair.

The honor system is alive and well at the untended self-serve **coconut stand** near Hana Highway's 48-mile marker.

HANA HIGHWAY NIGHTLIFE

Wunderbar (89 Hana Highway, Paia; 579-8808) usually has deejay music or live bands on Tuesday, Thursday, Friday and Saturday nights as well as Sunday afternoons. This local bar usually draws an upcountry crowd. Cover.

In the early evening, you can enjoy a duo singing Hawaiian music at the Hotel Hana Maui's **Paniolo Bar** (248-8211). As relaxed as Hana itself, this low-key establishment is always inviting.

HANA HIGHWAY BEACHES AND PARKS

H. A. Baldwin Park, a spacious county park about seven miles east of Kahului on the Hana Highway, is bordered by a playing field on one side and a crescent-shaped beach on the other. Palm and ironwood trees dot the half-mile-long beach. There's good shell collecting and a great view of West Maui. This otherwise lovely park has at times been the scene of robberies and violence. Tent camping is allowed on a quarter-acre meadow; a county permit is required. If you do camp here (which I do not recommend), exercise caution. The facilities include a picnic area complete with large pavilion, showers, restrooms and playground. The swimming is good, as is the bodysurfing, but beware of currents; the

---

SAILING HANA

The ultimate way to reach the luxurious pools of Oheo Gulch is via **Hana Hou Charters** *(Hana Bay; 877-7369). This 38-foot glass-bottomed boat will not only introduce you to one of the region's most exotic locales, but will also provide an opportunity to snorkel the offshore waters. If you'd prefer to keep your flippers dry, they also offer a sightseeing and photo cruise that includes a visit to Queen Kaahumanu's birthplace.*

Hookipa Beach Park is one of the prime windsurfing spots in the world.

snorkeling cannot be recommended. For surfing there are winter breaks, with a right slide. Fishing, for threadfin, mountain bass, goatfish and *ulua*, is good. To get to the park, turn left off Route 360, about seven miles east of Kahului.

For surfers and windsurfers, **Hookipa Beach Park** is one of the best spots on Maui. The beach itself is little more than a narrow rectangle of sand paralleled by a rocky shelf. Offshore, top-ranked windsurfers may be performing airborne stunts. On any day you're likely to see a hundred sails with boards attached skimming the whitecaps. The swimming is good only when the surf is low. The park is located on the Hana Highway about three miles east of Paia and offers picnic areas, restrooms and showers.

Honomanu Bay, a tranquil black-sand-and-rock beach surrounded by pandanus-covered hills and bisected by a stream, is a beautiful and secluded spot. There are no facilities, and the water is often too rough for swimming, but it's a favorite with surfers. The beach is located off of the Hana Highway (Route 360), about 30 miles east of Kahului. Turn off onto the dirt road located east of Kaumahina State Wayside; follow it to the beach.

Set in a heavenly seaside locale, **Waianapanapa State Park** is one of Hawaii's prettiest public facilities. The entire area is lush with tropical foliage and especially palmy pandanus trees. There's a black-sand beach, sea arches, a blowhole and two legendary caves. But pack your parkas; wind and rain are frequent. Just off the Hana Highway (Route 360) about four miles north of the town of Hana, it is a very popular spot. Swimming and snorkeling are both good—when the water is calm— and the fishing is good. There are campsites for up to 60 people on a grass-covered bluff overlooking the sea. The cabins are rented through the Division of State Parks (54 South High Street, Wailuku, Maui, HI 96793; 243-7389). These are plain but attractive accommodations renting on a sliding scale (starting at $10 single and $14 double up to $30 for six people). Each one contains a small bedroom with two bunk beds, plus a living room that can double as an extra bedroom. All cabins are equipped with bedding and complete kitchen facilities, and some have ocean views. A state permit is required. Other facilities here include a picnic area, restrooms and showers.

Tucked into a well-protected corner of Hana Bay, **Hana Beach Park** has a large pavilion and a curving stretch of sandy beach. As well as the picnic area, there are restrooms and showers and there is a snack bar

Hana's three police officers report that the region's number one crime is driving without a seatbelt.

across the street. It's a great place to meet local people. Swimming is good; snorkeling is good near the lighthouse, and surfers will find both summer and winter breaks on the north side of the bay; left slide. Bonefish, *ulua* and *papio* are routinely taken here and *moilii* run in the months of June and July.

Red Sand Beach, known to the Hawaiians as Kaihalulu ("roaring sea") Beach, is one of the most exotic and truly secluded beaches in all Hawaii. It is protected by lofty cliffs and can be reached only over a precarious trail. This is one place where going to the beach becomes a grand adventure. The beach is located on the far side of Kauiki Hill in Hana. Follow Uakea Road to its southern terminus. There is a grassy plot on the left between Hana School and the parking lot for the Hotel Hana Maui's sea ranch cottages. Here you will find a trail leading into the undergrowth. It traverses an overgrown Japanese cemetery and curves around Kauiki Hill, then descends precipitously to the beach. Be careful! A volcanic cinder beach, the sand is reddish in hue and coarse underfoot. Most dramatic of all is the lava barrier that crosses the mouth of this natural amphitheater, protecting the beach and creating an inshore pool. This is another beach popular with nudists. Swimming, snorkeling and fishing are all good. There are no facilities.

Hamoa Beach is at the head of Mokae Cove. A stretch of salt-and-pepper sand with rock outcroppings at each end, this strand is a pretty place, but the Hotel Hana Maui uses the beach as a semiprivate preserve. There are restrooms for guests and separate facilities for everybody else and a dining pavilion that is available only to guests, so a sense of segregation pervades the beach. To reach the place, follow the Hana Highway south from Hana for a little over a mile. Turn left on Haneoo Road and follow it for a mile to Hamoa.

More welcoming is **Koki Beach Park,** a sandy plot paralleled by a grassy park and half a mile back up the Haenoo Road toward the highway. Backdropped by lofty red cinder cliffs, Koki can be very windy and is plagued by currents. With a small island and sea arch offshore, it is also very pretty. There are restrooms and picnic areas here. Swimming is good, but exercise caution. There is good surfing at Hamoa and good bodysurfing at both beaches.

The stream that tumbles down Haleakala through **Oheo Gulch,** in the National Park's Kipahulu section (about ten miles south of Hana), forms several large pools and numerous small ones. The main pools, known to many as the **Seven Sacred Pools,** descend from above the

Hana Highway to the sea. This is a truly enchanting area swept by frequent wind and rain, and shadowed by Haleakala. It overlooks Maui's
rugged eastern shore. You can swim in the chilly waters and camp nearby. Primitive, meadow-style camping is available on a bluff above the
sea. No permit is required and there are no restrictions on the number of
occupants but there is a three-day limit. There are picnic facilities and
outhouses; bring your own drinking water.

NINE

Upcountry and Haleakala

Maui's Upcountry is a verdant mountainous belt that encircles Haleakala $\quad$ **157** along its middle slopes. Situated between coastline and crater rim, it's a region of ample rainfall and sparse population that is ideal for camping, hiking or just wandering. Here the flat fields of sugarcane and pineapples that blanket central Maui give way to open ranchland where curving hills are filled with grazing horses.

Farmers plant tomatoes, cabbages, carrots and the region's famous Maui onions. Proteas, those delicate flowers native to Australia and South Africa, grow in colorful profusion. Hibiscus, jacarandas and other wildflowers sweep along the hillsides like a rain storm. And on the region's two ranches—20,000-acre Haleakala Ranch and 30,000-acre Ulupalakua Ranch—Angus and Hereford cattle complete a picture far removed from Hawaii's tropical beaches.

Home to *paniolos*, Hawaii's version of the Western cowboy, the Upcountry region lies along the highways that lead to the crest of Haleakala crater. Route 37, Haleakala Highway, becomes the Kula Highway as it ascends to the Kula uplands. The **Church of the Holy Ghost** (12-mile marker), a unique octagonal chapel, was built here in 1897 for Portuguese immigrants working on Maui's ranches and farms.

This roadway angles southwest through Ulupalakua Ranch to the ruins of the **Makee Sugar Mill**, a once flourishing enterprise built in 1878. A currently flourishing business, **Tedeschi Winery** (878-6058), sits just across the road. Producing a pineapple wine called Maui Blanc, the winery rests in an old jailhouse built of lava and coral in 1857. Here at Hawaii's first winery you can stop for a taster's tour.

You can also turn up Route 377 to **Kula Botanical Gardens** (878-1715; admission). An excellent place for picnicking, the landscaped slopes contain an aviary, pond, "Taboo Garden" with poisonous plants and 40 varieties of protea, the flowering shrub that grows so beautifully in this region. Several farms, including **Sunrise Protea Farm** (Haleakala Crater Road; 878-2119), devoted primarily to proteas, are located nearby.

Another intriguing place is the tiny town of **Makawao**, where battered buildings and falsefront stores create an Old West atmosphere. This is the capital of Maui's cowboy country, similar to Waimea on the Big Island, with a rodeo every Fourth of July.

Just outside Makawao, a beautiful country estate dating from the early 1900s houses the **Hui No'eau Visual Arts Center** (2841 Baldwin Avenue; 572-6560). Local artists are often showcased in a gallery featuring changing exhibits. Art classes and a small shop are also a part of the center.

From Makawao the possibilities for exploring the Upcountry area are many. There are two **loop tours** I particularly recommend. The first climbs from town along Olinda Road (Route 390) past **Pookela Church** (572-8751), a coral sanctuary built in the 1843. It continues through a frequently rain-drenched region to the **Tree Growth Research Area**, jointly sponsored by state and federal forestry services. You can circle back down toward Makawao on Piiholo Road past the **University of Hawaii Agricultural Station**, where you will see more of the area's richly planted acreage.

The second loop leads down Route 365 to the Hana Highway. Turn left on the highway for several miles to Haiku Road, then head left along this country lane, which leads into overgrown areas, across one-lane bridges, past banana patches and through the tinroof town of **Haiku**.

UPCOUNTRY LODGING

A mountain lodge on the road to Haleakala Crater offers a cold-air retreat that is well-situated for anyone who wants to catch the sunrise over the crater. For years, **Kula Lodge** (878-1535) has rented Swiss chalets complete with fireplaces, sleeping lofts and sweeping views. The individual chalets are carpeted wall-to-wall and trimmed with stained-wood paneling. The central lodge features a cheery restaurant, bar and stone fireplace. An appealing mountain hideaway; ultra-deluxe.

Maui's premier gay retreat is **Camp Kula** (Kula; 878-2528), a spacious five-bedroom house that rests on seven acres where "HIV-positive guests are *always* welcome!" Located on the side of Haleakala at the 3000-foot level, it caters exclusively to gay men and women. Guests have full access to kitchen facilities, the living room and other features of the house. Budget to moderate.

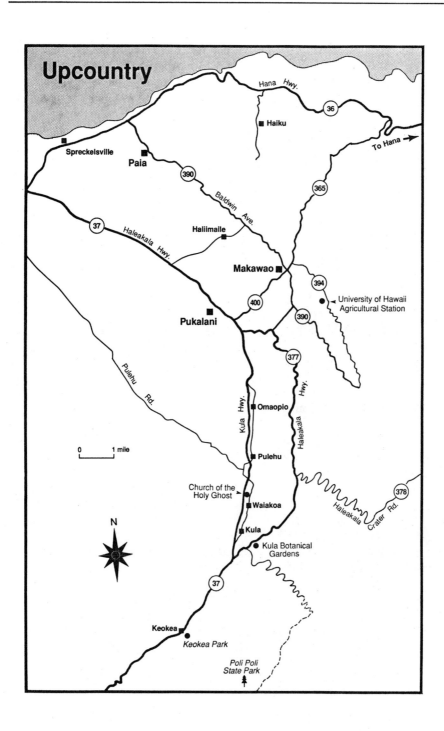

Upcountry

Surrounded by tropical jungle, the **Tea House Cottage Bed and Breakfast** (outside Haiku, one mile off Hana Highway; 572-5610) is a perfect retreat from the outside world. Filled with antiques and Oriental rugs, this one-bedroom cottage has a kitchen and a screened-in lanai. The grounds are full of flowering plants and trees, and paths lead to the ocean, a short walk away. Moderate.

UPCOUNTRY RESTAURANTS

There are several good dining spots in Pukalani Terrace Center in Pukalani on the Haleakala Highway. Among them is **Nick's Place** (572-8258), a breakfast-and-lunch-only cafeteria serving Japanese-Chinese-American fare. Choose from such à la carte items as *chow fun*, tempura, Portuguese sausage, stew or corned-beef hash. None are priced beyond the budget range, and several together comprise a hearty meal. At breakfast, try the eggs with Portuguese sausage.

A good local restaurant for breakfast or lunch is the **Up Country Café** (Haleakala Highway and Aewa Place, Pukalani; 572-2395). The theme here is bovine all the way, with the restaurant decked out in everything from cow bells to cow salt-and-pepper shakers. Breakfast is pretty predictable; lunch includes a half-dozen entrées such as beef curry stew, as well as such non-bovine fare as sautéed mahimahi and vegetarian lasagna. Budget.

For something a step more upscale, consider the **Makawao Steak House** (3612 Baldwin Avenue, Makawao; 572-8711). Knotty pine walls and a comfortable lounge lend the place an air of refined rusticity. The menu, popular among the upcountry gentry, is a mix of surf-and-turf dishes. Dinner only; deluxe.

In Makawao, you can go Mediterranean at **Casanova Italian Restaurant & Deli** (1188 Makawao Avenue; 572-0220), a stylish bistro that serves Italian-style seafood and pasta dishes at deluxe and moderate prices, respectively. For something faster, cheaper, and more casual, you can try the adjacent deli. The restaurant is closed on Sunday, but the deli is open seven days a week.

Or head across the street to **Polli's Mexican Restaurant** (1202 Makawao Avenue, Makawao; 572-7808). This sombreros-on-the-wall-and-oilcloth-on-the-tables eatery offers a full selection of Mexican dishes at moderate prices. A local gathering place popular with residents throughout Maui's Upcountry region, Polli's has become an institution over the years. It will inevitably be crowded with natives and tourists alike, all dining on tacos, burritos, tamales and tostadas.

Upcountry's contribution to the culinary revolution that has been sweeping Hawaii the past few years is **Haliimaile General Store** (900 Haliimaile Road, Haliimaile; 572-2666). A former plantation store that

Ulupalakua Ranch, covering 30,000 acres, is Maui's largest spread.

has been converted into a chic gathering place, it puts a creative spin on American cuisine and serves roast duckling, fresh island fish and beef from the Big Island at deluxe prices.

On the lower slope of Haleakala, **Kula Lodge Restaurant** (Haleakala Highway, Kula; 878-1535) enjoys a panoramic view of the island. Through picture windows you can gaze out on a landscape that rolls for miles to the sea. The exposed-beam ceiling and stone fireplace lend a homey feel, as do the homemade pastries. Specialties include rack of lamb, pasta dishes and such vegetarian entrées as spinach tofu pie. On the garden terrace, enjoy pizza and calzone baked in a wood-fired oven. Moderate to deluxe.

UPCOUNTRY SHOPPING

Baldwin Avenue in Makawao has developed over the years into a prime arts-and-crafts center. Housed in the falsefront stores that line the street you'll find galleries galore and a few boutiques besides.

The Courtyard (3620 Baldwin Avenue), an attractive woodframe mall, contains **Hot Island Glass** (572-4527), with a museum-quality collection of handblown glass pieces. Also here is **Viewpoints Gallery** (572-5979), which puts many of the higher-priced Lahaina galleries to shame.

The kids will love **Maui Child Toys & Books** (3643 Baldwin Avenue, Makawao; 572-2765), and women will find fashions by Upcountry designers at **Goodie's** (3633 Baldwin Avenue, Makawao; 572-0288). **Gecko Trading Company** (3621 Baldwin Avenue; 572-0249) is a small shop that also features contemporary fashions at reasonable prices. Both are enchanting spots in a town well worth exploring.

On the outskirts of Makawao, the 1917 Mediterranean-style Baldwin mansion is home to the **Hui Noeau Visual Arts Center** (2841 Baldwin Avenue; 572-6560). Here you can view rotating educational exhibits, purchase works by Maui artists or take the plunge yourself at one of the regular workshops on painting, printmaking, pottery, sculpture and much, much more.

In the Kula Lodge complex, the **Curtis Wilson Cost Gallery** (Haleakala Highway; 878-6544) sells lithographs and watercolors by well-known artists. The emphasis is on local landscapes and ocean scenery.

The Protea Gift Shoppe (Haleakala Highway, Kula; 878-6464) is an excellent place to find Maui's signature plant. In addition to exotic proteas, you can purchase locally made plumeria soap, macadamia nut butter and Maui onions.

UPCOUNTRY NIGHTLIFE

There are live bands on the weekends and disco music several week-nights at **Casanova Italian Restaurant** (1188 Makawao Avenue, Makawao; 572-0220). One of Upcountry's only nightspots, it features a range of live acts—from local Mauian to internationally known. Cover.

UPCOUNTRY PARKS

At the 6200-foot elevation on the slopes of Haleakala, the densely for-ested **Polipoli Spring State Recreation Area** is an ideal mountain retreat. Monterey and sugi pine, eucalyptus and Monterey cypress grow in stately profusion; not far from the campground there's a grove of redwoods. From Polipoli's ethereal heights you can look out over Cen-tral and West Maui, as well as the islands of Lanai, Molokai and Kahoo-lawe. Miles of trails, some leading up to Haleakala Crater, crisscross the park. From Kahului, take Haleakala Highway (Route 37) through Pu-kalani and past Waiakoa to Route 377. Turn left on 377 and follow it a short distance to the road marked for Polipoli. About half of this ten-mile road to the park is paved. The second half of the track is extremely rough and often muddy. It is advisable to take a four-wheel-drive vehicle.

Polipoli has a picnic area, restrooms and running water. There is meadow-style camping (a state permit is required) for up to 20 people; the cabin houses up to ten people and rents on a sliding scale from $10 single and $14 double up to $50 for ten people. The spacious cabin (three bedrooms) is sparsely furnished and lacks electricity. It does have a wood heating stove, gas cooking stove, gas lanterns, kitchen utensils and bedding. It can be rented from the Division of State Parks.

Keokea Park is a pleasant picnic spot on Route 37 in Keokea. There's a rolling lawn with picnic tables and restrooms.

Haleakala National Park

It seems only fitting that the approach to Haleakala Crater is along one of the world's fastest-climbing roads. From Kahului to the crater rim—a distance of 40 miles along Routes 37, 377 and 378—the macadam road rises from sea level to over 10,000 feet, and the silence is broken only by the sound of ears popping from the ascent.

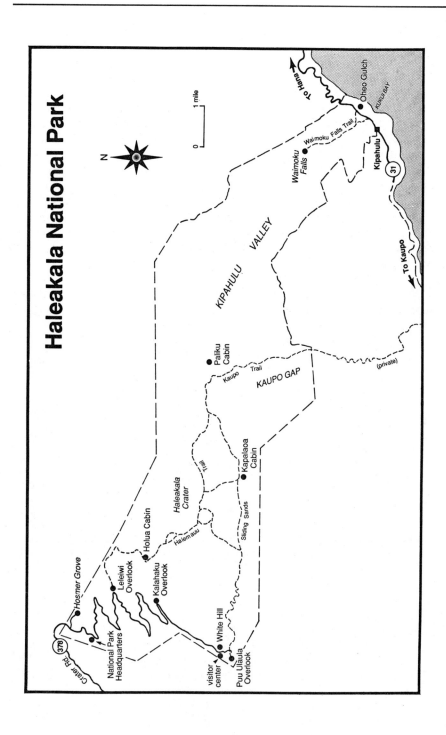

Haleakala National Park

At the crater lip, 10,023-feet in elevation, you look out over an awe-some expanse—seven miles long, over two miles wide, 21 miles around. This dormant volcano, which last erupted in 1790, is the central feature of a 27,284-acre national park that extends all the way through the Kipa-hulu Valley to the sea. The crater floor, 3000 feet below the rim, is a multihued wasteland filled with cinder cones, lava flows and mini-craters. It's a legendary place, with a mythic tradition that's as vital as its geologic history. It was from Haleakala ("House of the Sun") that the demigod Maui lassoed the sun and slowed its track across the sky to give his mother more daylight to dry her tapa cloth.

In the afternoon, the volcano's colors are most vivid, but during the morning the crater is more likely to be free of clouds. Before going up Haleakala, call 572-7749 or 871-5054 for a weather report. Then you can decide what time of day will be best for your explorations. Remember that it takes an hour-and-a half to two hours to reach the summit from Kahului, longer from the Kaanapali-Kapalua area. Be sure to bring warm clothes since the temperature drop from sea level to 10,000 feet can be 30° or more.

On the way up to the crater you'll pass **Hosmer Grove** (6800-feet), a picnic area and campground surrounded by eucalyptus, spruce, juniper and cedar trees.

National Park Headquarters (572-9306), located at the 7030-foot elevation, contains an information desk and maps, and makes a good starting point. Be sure to see the Hawaiian state bird, the *nene*, a rare species of Hawaiian goose, located in a pen adjacent to the center.

The first crater view comes at **Leleiwi Overlook**, an 8800-foot perch from which you'll be able to see all the way from Hana across the island to Kihei. Here at sunset, under correct meteorological conditions, you can see your shadow projected on the clouds and haloed by a rainbow. To experience this "Specter of the Brocken," stand atop the crater rim looking toward the cloud-filled crater with the setting sun at your back.

LATE SLEEPERS, TAKE NOTE

One of Maui's favorite tourist rituals is a predawn trip to the top of Haleakala to watch the sun rise. Unfortunately, the weather can be foggy and cold. Besides that, getting up early is probably the last thing you want to do on vacation. If so, consider the alternative: Sleep late, take your time getting to the top, and arrive in time for sunset. But, then again, you'll miss a dazzling, almost religious experience. Call 871-5054 or 572-7749 to check on the weather before making the trip up!

Up the hill, a side road leads to **Kalahaku Overlook**, a 9324-foot aerie that offers a unique view of several cinder cones within the crater. Just below the parking lot are numerous **silverswords**. Related to sunflowers, these spike-leaved plants grow only on Maui and the Big Island. They remain low bristling plants for up to 20 years before blooming into a flowering stalk. Each plant blossoms once, sometime between May and November, and then dies.

The best view of the crater is farther up the road at the **Haleakala Visitor Center**, 9745-feet elevation, where you'll find an information desk, as well as a series of exhibits about the volcano. From this vantage point you can gaze out toward Koolau Gap to the north and Kaupo Gap to the south. Several peaks located along the crater rim loom out of the clouds; cinder cones, including 1000-foot Puu o Maui, rise up from the crater floor.

From the visitor center a short trail heads up to **White Hill**. Composed of andesite lava and named for its characteristic light color, this mound is dotted with stone windbreaks once used as sleeping places by Hawaiians who periodically visited the summit of Haleakala.

It's a short drive to the crater summit at **Puu Ulaula Overlook**. From the plate-glass lookout you can view the Big Island, Molokai, Lanai, West Maui and the crater itself. On an extremely clear day this 360° panorama may even include a view of Oahu, 130 miles away.

Perched high above atmospheric haze and the lights of civilization, Haleakala is also an excellent spot for stargazing. If you can continue to the end of Skyline Drive, past the **Haleakala Observatory**, you'll see that it is also an important center for satellite tracking and television communications.

While the views along the crater rim are awesome, the best way to see Haleakala is from the inside looking out. With 36 miles of hiking trails, two campsites and three cabins, the crater provides a tremendous opportunity for explorers. Within the belly of this monstrous volcano, you'll see such geologic features as cinder cones, lava tubes and spatter vents. The Hawaiians marked their passing with stone altars, shelters and adze quarries. You may also spy the rare nene (a Hawaiian relative of the Canada goose), as well as chukar partridges, pheasants, mynahs and white-tailed tropicbirds.

The crater floor is a unique environment, one of constant change and unpredictable weather. Rainfall varies from 12 inches annually in the southwestern corner to 200 inches at Paliku. Temperatures, usually hovering between 55° and 75° during daylight, may fall below freezing at night. Campers should come prepared with warm clothing and sleeping gear, a tent, poncho, lantern and stove (no open fires are permitted). Don't forget the sunblock, as the elevation on the crater bottom averages 6700 feet and the ultraviolet radiation is intense.

Within the crater you can explore three main trails. **Sliding Sands Trail**, a steep cinder and ash path, begins near the Haleakala Visitor Center. It descends from the crater rim along the south wall to Kapalaoa cabin, then on to Paliku cabin. In the course of this ten-mile trek, the trail drops over 3000 feet. From Paliku, the **Kaupo Trail** leaves the crater through Kaupo Gap and descends to the tiny town of Kaupo, eight miles away on Maui's southeast coast. **Halemauu Trail** (8 miles) begins from the road three-and-a-half miles beyond National Park Headquarters and descends 1400 feet to the crater floor. It passes Holua cabin and eventually joins Sliding Sands Trail near the Paliku cabin.

There are campgrounds at **Holua** and **Paliku** that require a permit from National Park Headquarters. Permits are given out on a first-come, first-served basis (not available in advance), so plan accordingly. The campgrounds have pit toilets and running water. Camping is limited to two days at one site and three days total at both. There is also a 12-person cabin at each campsite and at **Kapalaoa**. Equipped with wood stoves, pit toilets, cooking utensils and mattresses, these primitive facilities are extremely popular. So popular, in fact, that guests are chosen by lottery three months in advance. For more information, write Haleakala National Park, P.O. Box 369, Makawao, Maui, HI 96768, or call 572-9306.

Index

About the Author and Illustrator

Ray Riegert is the author of eight travel books, including *Hidden San Francisco and Northern California*. His most popular work, *Hidden Hawaii*, won both the coveted Lowell Thomas Travel Journalism Award and the Hawaii Visitors Bureau Award for Best Guidebook. In addition to his role as publisher of Ulysses Press, he has written for the *Chicago Tribune, Saturday Evening Post, San Francisco Examiner & Chronicle* and *Travel & Leisure*. A member of the Society of American Travel Writers, he lives in the San Francisco Bay Area with his wife, travel publisher Leslie Henriques, and their son Keith and daughter Alice.

Sandra Wong received her bachelor of fine arts degree at the San Francisco Art Institute. Her work has been shown in Los Angeles, San Francisco and China. She currently lives in Oakland, California, where she is preparing for an upcoming show of her work.

HIDDEN GUIDES

Adventure travel or a relaxing vacation?—"Hidden" guidebooks are the only travel books in the business to provide detailed information on both. Aimed at environmentally aware travelers, our motto is "Adventure Travel Plus." These books combine details on unique hotels, restaurants and sightseeing with information on camping, sports and hiking for the outdoor enthusiast.

ULTIMATE GUIDES

These innovative guides present the best and most unique features of a destination. Quality is the keynote. They are as likely to cover a mom-and-pop café as a gourmet restaurant, a quaint bed and breakfast as a five-star tennis resort. In addition to thoroughly covering each destination, they feature short articles and one-line "teasers" that are both fun and informative.

THE NEW KEY GUIDES

Based on the concept of ecotourism, The New Key Guides are dedicated to the preservation of Central America's rare and endangered species, architecture and archaeology. Filled with helpful tips, they give travelers everything they need to know about these exotic destinations.

VIRAGO WOMAN'S TRAVEL GUIDES

Written through a woman's eye and steeped in the grand tradition of travel literature, these guides speak directly to the special interests of solo travelers, businesswomen and women traveling with children. Each title offers a fascinating blend of practical information and cultural insights. History, art and contemporary society are examined from a woman's point of view with fascinating results.

ULYSSES PRESS To order direct, send a check or money order to: Ulysses Press, P.O. Box 3440, Berkeley, CA 94703-3440; to charge by credit card, call 800/377-2542 or 510/601-8301.

TRAVEL

_____ Hidden Coast of California, $14.95

_____ Hidden Florida, $14.95

_____ Hidden Florida Keys and Everglades, $9.95

_____ Hidden Hawaii, $15.95

_____ Hidden Mexico, $13.95

_____ Hidden New England, $14.95

_____ Hidden Pacific Northwest, $14.95

_____ Hidden San Francisco and Northern California, $14.95

_____ Hidden Southern California, $14.95

_____ Hidden Southwest, $15.95

_____ Disneyland and Beyond: The Ultimate Family Guidebook, $9.95

_____ Disney World and Beyond: The Ultimate Family Guidebook, $10.95

_____ Florida's Gold Coast: The Ultimate Guidebook, $8.95

_____ Ultimate Las Vegas and Beyond, $9.95

_____ The Maya Route: The Ultimate Guidebook, $14.95

_____ Ultimate Arizona, $11.95

_____ Ultimate California, $14.95

_____ Ultimate Santa Fe and Beyond, $11.95

_____ Ultimate Washington, $11.95

_____ The New Key to Belize, $13.95

_____ The New Key to Cancún and the Yucatán, $13.95

_____ The New Key to Costa Rica, $14.95

_____ The New Key to Panama, $13.95

_____ The Virago Woman's Travel Guide to New York, $13.95

_____ The Virago Woman's Travel Guide to Paris, $13.95

_____ The Virago Woman's Travel Guide to Rome, $13.95

FREE SHIPPING!

Total cost of books   = _____

Book rate shipping   = __FREE__

California residents add 8% sales tax.   = _____

                                    Total enclosed = _____

NAME _____PHONE _____

ADDRESS_____

CITY _____STATE ____ZIP _____